UT HISTORY
101

For Doreas and Bill —
My dear friends,
neighbors and keepers!
Forever hook-'em!
Margaret Berry

11/10/97

UT HISTORY 101

Highlights in the History of The University of Texas at Austin

MARGARET CATHERINE
BERRY

Illustrations by Mark Mitchell

EAKIN PRESS ★ AUSTIN, TEXAS

FIRST EDITION

Published in the United States of America
By Eakin Press
A Division of Sunbelt Media, Inc.
P.O. Drawer 90159
Austin, Tx 78709

2 3 4 5 6 7 8 9

ISBN 1-57168-188-4

Library of Congress Cataloging-in-Publication Data

Berry, Margaret Catherine.
    UT history 101 : highlights in the history of the University of Texas at
Austin / by Margaret C. Berry.
        p.   cm.
    Includes bibliographical references and index.
    ISBN 1-57168-188-4   .
    1. University of Texas at Austin--History.   I. Title.
LD5333.B444 1997
378.764'31--dc21
                                              97-14498
                                              CIP

Dedicated to

The memory of my parents,
Mr. and Mrs. Winfred Berry,
for oh, so many reasons, among them being

(1) they gave me continuous love and support, and
(2) they permitted me to choose The University of Texas.

CONTENTS

The West Wing of Old Main, 1884-1889.

PREFACE

This little book is for those who want to know about The University of Texas, yet who don't have time to read all that has been written about it. It is for all orange-bloods who love the place and often find themselves in a corner when trying to answer questions about its history.

The book is short, and making it so wasn't easy for one who tends to be wordy when talking about the University. I've tried to select *highlights* in the University's rich history and development. At a great university important events occur daily: administrative decisions, significant research findings, legislation and court rulings, unexpected events, and on and on. What I consider to be highlights might differ from those selected by another person. Each time I've selected an entry, I've asked myself, "Is this really a highlight? Was this event important in making the University what it is today?" The result has been that I've discarded numerous entries. On the other hand, I've awakened in the middle of the night remembering something omitted that is truly a highlight. No doubt there are others.

Therefore, these selections are mine; each reader might have different priorities. Perhaps the omissions and inclusions will stimulate good conversation about the University. I hope you will find the ones I've selected helpful in giving you a better understanding of the University's rich history.

Here's what I've done. In Part I, I've described highlights in the growth and development of the University as separate entries. I've tried to arrange them in (well, almost) chronological order so that the historical flow will not be too jumpy; nevertheless, it remains jumpy because of brevity and omissions. (Remember, I was trying to keep it all brief.) The italicized portions are my attempt to bring up-to-date some of the entries so that a minimal amount of repetition is avoided.

Part II was more fun and will probably be more interesting to the reader. In very short accounts, I've attempted to describe the student culture of each decade in the University's history. I've used a different format because this latter style is easier to read and adequately serves the purpose. Part I entries needed more explanation.

It is not easy to separate "student culture" from "growth and development." The student culture, of course, heavily influences the development of a university and even makes it unique. I've kept this consideration in mind and included a few entries in Part I that needed fuller description. For even fuller description of any of the items, numerous sources are available on campus in the University Archives at the Center for American History in Sid Richardson Hall.

Three readers of the manuscript deserve a standing ovation. They are Dr. Ronald M. Brown, Richard Pennington, and James R. Raup. All three made very helpful suggestions that improved the final draft. I am grateful for their assistance and their friendship. Any errors you find, however, are mine. John A. Adkins, a former student and good friend, encouraged me to proceed with the idea for a book. I believe he even named it before it was written. Thanks, John. I am also grateful to Edwin A. Eakin and Eakin Press for publishing this book, a companion to the first book I wrote twenty years ago, *UT Austin: Traditions and Nostalgia*, which is still in print.

Material herein, unavoidably, is drawn partially from other books I've written about the University. I hope the reader will gain pleasure and knowledge from this little book. It is designed so that you can open it to any page and, hopefully, find an interesting fact or two about a great University.

Enjoy, and forever hook 'em!

MARGARET C. BERRY
April 1997

INTRODUCTION

The University of Texas at Austin is a major comprehensive research university with a broad mission for undergraduate and graduate education, research, and public service. Administrators today say that it fulfills its constitutional mandate to be a "university of the first class," while "challenging its faculty and students to seek new knowledge and greater understanding of an ever-changing, multicultural society."

As the academic flagship of the University System's fifteen component institutions, UT Austin has come a long way from its beginning in 1883. Today, its contiguous main campus has more than 350 acres; it has over 48,000 students, 2,300-plus faculty and almost 15,000 staff members. Also a part of UT Austin is the 477-acre J. J. "Jake" Pickle Research Campus, eight miles north of the main campus; the 445-acre Brackenridge Tract bordering Town Lake; and the 94-acre Montopolis Research Center in southeast Austin. In addition, the University owns the McDonald Observatory on Mt. Locke in West Texas, the Marine Science Institute at Port Aransas, the Winedale Historical Center near Round Top, the Bee Cave Research Center west of Austin, Paisano (the J. Frank Dobie ranch) near Austin, and the Sam Rayburn Library near Bonham.

The current faculty includes the winners of the 1948 Pulitzer Prize in Fiction, the 1967 Pulitzer Prize in History, the 1977 Nobel Prize in Chemistry, and the 1979 Nobel Prize in Physics. In addition, dozens of faculty members have been selected to membership in prestigious scholarly organizations.

The student population has become increasingly diverse. Students come from all fifty states and over one hundred countries. The University attracts large numbers of academically talented students in all fields. In 1995 UT enrolled 754 Merit Scholars, and the average Scholastic Aptitude Test (SAT) score for freshmen who enrolled in

1995 was 1217, more than 205 points higher than the national average of all college-bound high school seniors.

Austin, the state capital, has been touted as one of the most pleasant places to live in the United States. Its metropolitan population is approximately one million people. Located on the Colorado River at the edge of the beautiful Texas Hill Country, Austin's Town Lake, numerous parks, hike and bike trails, libraries, and recreational and cultural events make it a highly desirable location for the University.

The history of The University of Texas reflects the long struggle of the people of the state to provide public education for its citizens. But this isn't UT's only goal. To be a major research university, the combined talents of citizens, including faculty, staff, and students, never cease to explore ways to enhance development. The University's history reveals how continuous change has affected academic development and student culture.

PART I

GROWTH AND DEVELOPMENT OF THE UNIVERSITY

GROWTH AND DEVELOPMENT

The idea to establish a university in Texas was not new when members of the constitutional convention of 1876 adopted the current Constitution of Texas. The origin of The University of Texas dates back to at least 1827 when Article 216 of the 1827 *Constitucion de Coahuila y Tejas* provided that "seminaries most required for affording the public the means of instruction in the sciences and arts useful to the state" should be established. No action was taken to implement the provision.

Leaders of the Texas Revolution decreed, therefore, in the Declaration of Independence, March 2, 1836, that Mexico "has failed to establish any public system of education" as one of the reasons for revolt. And then, in the same year stated in the new Constitution of the Republic of Texas: "It shall be the duty of Congress, as soon as circumstances will permit, to provide by law, a general system of education."

The first official suggestion for an institution of university rank occurred in a bill introduced by Kelsey A. Douglass on November 20, 1837. At the Second Congress of the Republic of Texas, meeting in Houston in an unroofed frame building on a cold, rainy day, he proposed a bill to incorporate The University of Texas. Nothing was enacted into law at the time. Nevertheless, The University of Texas was the part of our education system first to receive attention in the Congress of the Republic.

President Mirabeau B. Lamar of the new Republic of Texas spoke of the need for education and for a university when he made his first speech to the Texas Congress on

December 20, 1838. His words are an important part of the intellectual history of Texas:

> Education is a subject in which every Citizen, especially every parent, feels a deep and lively concern . . . . It is admitted by all, that [a] cultivated mind is the guardian genius of democracy, and, while guided and controlled by virtue, is the noblest attribute of man. It is the only dictator that freemen acknowledge and the only security which freemen desire . . . . Let me therefore urge it upon you, gentlemen, not to postpone this matter too long . . . . Postpone it a few years, and millions will be necessary to accomplish the great design.

The resolution of Kelsey Douglass at the Second Congress of the Republic of Texas grew eventually to become a law introduced by Ezekiel W. Cullen on January 26, 1839, at the Third Congress. Cullen's original bill provided for twenty leagues of land "to be set apart and appropriated for the establishment and endowment of two colleges or universities, one to be established in the Eastern and the other in the Western part of Texas." The bill was amended to read "fifty leagues of land" and was passed. It was from this original land grant that the major part of the University's Permanent Fund is derived today.

The naming of the present campus "College Hill" is partly a matter of legend. It is certain, however, that an act locating the capital of Texas was passed on January 14, 1839, and that when the streets were laid out, forty acres almost a mile north of the proposed location of the new Capitol were designated as "College Hill."

Two decades later Gov. E. M. Pease, in his retiring message to the convening Seventh Legislature, urged that speed be used in passing measures for the establishment of a state university. On February 11, 1858, after delay and a considerable amount of opposition, "A Bill to Establish The University of Texas" was passed and signed the next day by Governor Pease.

Legislators wrote into the measure: "From the earliest times, it has been the cherished design of the people of the Republic and of the State of Texas, that there shall be established . . . an institution of learning for the education of the youth of the land in the higher branches of learning and in the liberal arts and sciences . . . ." The measure set aside for [one] university (1) "the sum of one hundred thousand dollars of the United States bonds in the Treasury not otherwise appropriated" and (2) the fifty leagues of land reserved for education in 1839, and (3) one section out of every ten set apart in 1858 to encourage construction of railroads in Texas.

This Act of 1858 was never implemented because Gov. Sam Houston did not believe sufficient funds were available for the upkeep of a university and because the Civil War ensued and part of the money was used for war expenses.

After the Civil War, the Texas Legislature voted to replace all university funds that had been borrowed, if the Constitution of Texas of 1866 would provide for the maintenance of the university fund and would direct the Legislature to make provisions by law "at an early day" for the organization and operation of a university. The Constitution met the challenge; even so, the state took no action for the next fifteen years although boards of administrators were appointed from 1866 to 1873.

The Legislature took advantage of the Morrill Act (1862) passed by Congress and established the

Agricultural and Mechanical College of Texas in 1871 at College Station on the Brazos River. Still, the College, designated as a branch of the University, did not open until the fall of 1876.

The Constitution of 1876 incorporated a provision that was little more than a confirmation of the Act of 1858 to establish a university. The state took away from the endowment the railroad lands that had been added to it by the original act, but it designated one million acres of unappropriated public domain in West Texas (and in 1883 added another one million) with the income from sale of grazing rights on the land to go to The University of Texas and its branches (the Agricultural and Mechanical College, a "university for the instruction of the colored youths of the state," and the Medical Branch). The Constitution also contained a direction that the University be "an institution of the first class."

On March 30, 1881, the Texas Legislature passed "An Act to Establish the University of Texas," the so-called "Enabling Act." It ordered a statewide election for the purpose of locating the University, the creation of a Board of Regents of eight members to be nominated by the governor, with the advice and consent of the Senate, and the Act defined the Regents' duties. It also stipulated that admission fees should never exceed thirty dollars, and that the University should enroll male and female on equal terms without charge for tuition; that religious qualifications for admission to any office or privilege of the University should be banned, and that no course of a sectarian character should be taught. O. M. Roberts was governor at the time the enabling legislation was passed.

Governor Roberts proclaimed an election to be held on September 6, 1881, for the purpose of locating The University of Texas. Despite an extensive campaign of about ten other communities, the results placed the Medical Branch at Galveston and the Main University at Austin. Tyler, Waco, and Thorp Springs were runners-up for the Main campus. A. P. Wooldridge, Dudley Goodall Wooten, and Alexander W. Terrell were leaders in capturing the vote for Austin. The results were announced on October 17, 1881.

Two days after he signed the Act of Establishment of the University, Governor Roberts nominated eight men to serve as Regents: Judge Thomas J. Devine of Bexar County; Dr. Ashbel Smith of Harris; Richard B. Hubbard of Smith; A. N. Edwards of Hopkins; Prof. Smith Ragsdale of Parker; E. M. Pease of Travis; James W. Throckmorton of Cullen; and Dr. James H. Starr of Harrison. Objections were voiced concerning the appointment of former Governor Pease, and he withdrew before the Senate acted; James H. Bell of Travis was nominated in his place. Governor Throckmorton and Dr. Starr resigned before the first meeting, and their places were filled by Judge T. M. Harwood of Gonzalez and Judge J. S. Camp of Upshur.

"In the appointment of the Regents," wrote Governor Roberts later, "I had . . . sought gentlemen of ability and learning, who had held public positions, and whose reputation would inspire confidence in the performance of the duties of the position which they had been appointed to occupy."

The Governor convened the Regents for the first time in Austin on November 15, 1881. Dr. Ashbel Smith, one of the most distinguished citizens of Texas at the time, was elected president (not called chairman until later) of the Board of Regents. All were present except Judge Camp. The historic meeting took place in the Governor's private office in the Temporary Capitol (the old Capitol had burned earlier that month).

Note: The University is now governed by a board of nine regents elected from different areas of the state, nominated by the governor, and appointed with the advice and consent of the Senate. The general charge of the University is extended to the General Faculty, subject to the supervision of the UT System Board of Regents and the authority it has vested in administrative officers.

The new Regents selected an architect named Frederick Ernst Ruffini. From the Cleveland, Ohio area, he had moved to Austin in 1877 and had designed and supervised the construction of the Millet Opera House (now the Austin Club), the Texas School for the Deaf, and the Hancock Building. He was popular as a designer of courthouses; those in Corsicana, San Marcos, Georgetown, Sulphur Springs, Quitman, Blanco, Henderson, Franklin, and Longview were designed by him. Even though funds were not available to construct all of the building, Ruffini designed the entire structure.

The Regents had to limit construction to only one-third of the building, the West Wing, and a contract for its construction was awarded to Abner Hugh Cook, who had lived in Austin since 1839. He had already built the Governor's Mansion, Woodlawn (for Governor Pease), and the Neill-Cochran House.

Dr. Ashbel Smith led the effort to recruit the best men available so that the University might have a recognized reputation for scholarship. He thought a good faculty

7

should come first; gymnasiums, residence halls, and even administrators could come later. Modeled after the University of Virginia, the University had no president for its first twelve years. The faculty chose a chairman, J. W. Mallet, to guide it loosely and do the necessary paper work. The Regents served in a supervisory capacity and held the primary responsibility.

Oscar Henry Cooper, 1872 graduate of Yale, who had no official capacity with the University, made the establishment of the University his special project. He joined Dr. Smith in urging selection of a scholarly faculty without regard to political or religious beliefs. Both Cooper and Smith worked at their own expense to make the University a success.

The cornerstone for the Main Building was laid at noon on November 17, 1882, one day after the scheduled ceremony because of cold, rainy weather. Dr. Ashbel Smith, president of the Board of Regents, presided and made the dedicatory address, and also laid the cornerstone with the assistance of the Masonic Order and other societies. In his address, Dr. Smith said, both metaphorically and prophetically, "Smite the rocks with the rod of knowledge, and fountains of unstinted wealth will gush forth."

The first meeting of the faculty was held on May 17, 1883, not in Austin but in the historic Maxwell House in Nashville, Tennessee. Why? Nashville was a more convenient place for the men to meet (all lived east of the Mississippi River), and besides, Dr. Smith was afraid all would resign when they saw the feeble preparations that had been made in Austin.

Those present were Dr. Smith, who called the meeting, and the newly elected professors of the Academic

Department of the University: Leslie Waggener, J. W. Mallet, Milton W. Humphreys, and Leroy Broun. After drawing up "The Preliminary Announcement of the University of Texas at Austin," the meeting adjourned to meet next in Austin on June 4 and 5, 1883.

On September 11, 1883, The University of Texas officially opened and announced itself ready to register any students who might appear with the necessary qualifications.

The University experienced delays in construction of the Main Building, and it was obvious that the building would not be ready for classes in September. Gov. John Ireland granted permission to the faculty and the Regents to use the Temporary Capitol at the southwest corner of Congress Avenue and Eleventh Street during the fall, and to erect temporary partitions within it to make lecture rooms.

Smith Ragsdale, who had resigned as a member of the Board of Regents, was elected as the first Proctor, the only non-teaching staff member that first year. He reported that a sufficient number of accommodations (both room and board) for all prospective students were available at twenty dollars per month.

The Academic and Law departments were organized first, and registration continued throughout the fall. The first student to matriculate was Samuel Jackson Sheffield from Lodi, in Marion County, who enrolled in the Law Department. Jessie Andrews of Austin was the first woman to enroll; she entered the Academic Department.

On September 15, the University held opening ceremonies in the unfinished West Wing of the Main Building. A crowd of about two hundred attended the morning ceremonies and heard stirring addresses by Dr. Ashbel Smith, Prof. John William Mallet, Gov. John Ireland, and former Gov. Oran M. Roberts. Dr. Smith noted the potential importance of the new university for Texas and its neighboring territories.

When classes began eight men, all "good southern Democrats," made up the entire faculty. Other than those who attended the first meeting in Nashville were Robert L. Dabney, Henri Tallichet, Oran M. Roberts, and Robert S. Gould. Registration reached approximately one hundred students by the opening day, but by the end of the first year, two hundred and twenty-one students (one hundred and sixty-three men and, remarkably, fifty-eight women) had registered; one hundred and sixty-nine enrolled in the Academic Department and fifty-two in the Law Department. At the first commencement, held in the Millet Opera House on June 14, 1884, thirteen law students received degrees.

Professor Mallet, who returned to Virginia after the first year, wrote later, "Among the most vivid impressions that remain to me of those days is that of the Texas spirit that seemed to say — 'Yes, it is not very clear how the thing is to be done, but the State of Texas has said it shall be done, and it *will* be done, somehow.' "

Capt. James B. Clark succeeded Smith Ragsdale as Proctor at the end of the first year, and Helen Marr Kirby was appointed "Lady Assistant." These two individuals were the only non-teaching staff members until a president was appointed in 1895. Clark's work included duties that might have been performed by registrar, comptroller, auditor, dean of students, librarian, grounds keeper, and secretary to the Regents. He served the University until he died on campus in 1908. Kirby, whose title was changed to Dean of Women in 1903 after construction of the Woman's Building, exerted immeasurable influence on the campus culture. A proper Victorian, she insisted that young women at the University should act and dress like ladies — at all times.

The Alumni Association of The University of Texas (now the Ex-Students' Association) was organized on June 17, 1885, which was Commencement Day at the end of the University's second year. The small group of alumni — thirteen lawyers who graduated in 1884 and twenty-one lawyers and one academic of the class of 1885 — met in the still incomplete wing of the University building, adopted a constitution, and elected officers. Membership at first was open only to persons who had graduated from the University. The first president was J. L. Stone of Paris, Texas.

In 1889 the University received from the 21st Legislature its first appropriation from the general revenue fund. Walter Grisham introduced the bill, approved on April 8, which was significant in the history of the University. This appropriation of $25,000 was for the 1889-1891 biennium.

The 22nd Legislature in 1891 expressed more confidence by appropriating for the Main University a total of $60,000 and for the Medical Branch a total of $74,000 out of the general revenue and an "indemnity fund." Gov. Lawrence S. Ross, in his farewell address in 1891, urged: "To insure . . . success [the University] must have an adequate permanent endowment fund that will give a certainty and uniformity of income upon which its Regents can always rely and relieve the Legislature of the contests which usually attend the passage of . . . appropriations." Gov. James S. Hogg, in his inaugural address the same year, said: "The Constitution requires the Legislature to provide for the maintenance, support and direction of [the University] so that it shall be first class . . . ."

President H. Y. Benedict later wrote: "Slowly, slowly,

thus was the habit of making appropriations for higher education formed."

Not until 1888 did the legislature provide for the establishment of the Medical Branch, even though Galveston had been voted the site in 1881. The legislative provision was made on the condition that the city donate a block of land, and that the Sealy estate build and give a hospital to the school. The will of the elder John Sealy had already empowered the executors of his estate to transfer the hospital, for which he left a bequest, to the University if the Medical Branch were established in Galveston. The John Sealy Hospital was completed and turned over to the University in 1891. This was the first of countless benefactions from the Sealy family that made the development of the Medical Branch possible.

During the summer and fall of 1891, the old Chemical Laboratory [which burned in 1926] was built on the campus near the site of the current Biological Laboratory. This marked the beginning of the University's long and distinguished history as a leader and innovator in scientific research.

On February 13, 1895, the legislature transferred control of University lands to the Regents of The University of Texas. Under state control, the two million acres of land had yielded the University only $74,000 in twelve years. The bill to make the change was introduced by Senator J. M. Pressler.

After twelve years with a Chairman of the Faculty as the chief executive officer of the University, the Regents decided in 1895 to select a president.

Leslie Waggener, a native of Kentucky and a graduate of Bethel College and Harvard Law School, had served as chairman of the faculty from 1884 until 1894 and was appointed president *ad interim* for the school year 1895-1896; he died on August 19, 1896.

Note: Beginning with Waggener, the University has had twenty-seven presidents (to 1997), with tenure averaging about four years. Waggener (counting his years as chairman of the faculty), Harry Yandell Benedict, and Harry H. Ransom have had the longest periods of tenure. For a complete list of the presidents, see the appendix.

The original Main Building was the first building on the campus. Although the cornerstone was laid in 1882, the entire building was not completed until 1899. (The West Wing was completed in January 1884; the middle portion, including the auditorium, was opened in 1889; and the East Wing was completed in 1899.) The walls of the auditorium reverberated with oratory and exhortations of former governors of Texas, President Theodore Roosevelt, William Jennings Bryan, and Helen Keller, and with the celebrated singing of Alma Gluck, Madam Schumann-Heinck, and John McCormack. Stark Young's Curtain Club plays and even Carrie Nation's hatchet-throwing entertained students.

Draped in ivy imported from England, Old Main was the symbol for the University to students who attended before it was razed in 1935. Its untuneful Tower chimes, added in 1930, pealed out the hour to the University community. They were a gift to the University by Albert Sidney Burleson, an 1884 UT law graduate, who had been US Postmaster General under President Woodrow Wilson. (They are now the beautiful, but still untuneful, bells on the pylons near Bass Concert Hall.)

Belonging to this same period of University history were old B. Hall, the first campus dormitory; the old Chemistry Building that burned in 1926; the Woman's Building that burned in 1959; the old Law Building (razed in 1972); and the old Engineering Building, still standing, renamed the Gebauer Building.

Most universities and colleges have a school song. University students, during the early years, gathered on the front steps of Old Main at sunset and sang familiar songs.

In 1903 at a fund-raiser for the track team at the old Hancock Theater downtown, lyrics for a song to the tune of "I've been working on the railroad" were sung for the first time. John Lang Sinclair, a student poet, hurriedly wrote the song that was sung by a quartet and received the cheers of all in the theater. "The Eyes of Texas" eventually, after years, became the official University song. The words were a take-off on the often-stated words of then president, W. L. Prather, "Students, the eyes of Texas are upon you!" This statement itself was a take-off on the words of Robert E. Lee, who often spoke to the young men at Washington College, when Prather was a student: "Young men, the eyes of the South are upon you!"

Note: The framed original copy of "The Eyes of Texas" now hangs in the Alumni Center on the campus. Another copy, a silk-screen, was taken to the moon in 1969 by University ex-student Alan L. Bean. This prized copy is also at the Alumni Center.

University officials and professors worked for high academic standards from the beginning. Through its affiliated schools program, summer schools, and extension work, the University encouraged young people throughout the state to further their education. Beginning in 1884 graduates of "affiliated" high schools, if at least sixteen years of age, could enter the University without taking entrance examinations; graduates of unaffiliated high schools could enter if they passed certain entrance examinations. Through the years, admission requirements gradually have been raised.

Even though William P. Hunnicutt had graduated in 1885 with a Bachelor of Science and a major in engineering, there was no Department of Engineering until later. Thomas Ulvan Taylor came to the University in 1888 as an adjunct professor of applied mathematics. Between 1888 and 1894, twelve graduates received degrees with majors in civil engineering. The Department (later called College) of Engineering was inaugurated in 1894, with Taylor as dean. The Department was first located on the fourth floor of the middle section of Old Main. An Engineering Building (now the Gebauer Building) was not constructed until 1904.

A number of academic changes took place at the turn of the century. The following were some of the signs of growth and development:

A summer session was first conducted in 1898. President William L. Prather (1899-1905) gave special attention to raising academic standards. New degree requirements, including more rigid entrance policies, went into effect. New courses, incorporating new methods, were added to the curriculum. The School (now College) of Education was organized in 1805 and received acclaim throughout the state.

On April 28, 1905, a chapter of Phi Beta Kappa was formally installed on the University campus. News that a charter had been granted was received the proceeding fall when a letter explained that out of nineteen applications, The University of Texas was one of ten that had been approved.

The faculty passed the first regulations concerning scholastic probation in 1903 and authorized strict regulations concerning class attendance in 1904.

The Texas Academy of Science (1892) and the Texas State Historical Association (1897) were active organizations and held regular meetings on the campus.

The University celebrated its twenty-fifth anniversary in 1908 as Sidney Edward Mezes was inaugurated as president. Mezes succeeded David Franklin Houston, who left to become chancellor of Washington University in St. Louis. At the same time, the original Law Building (razed in 1972) was dedicated.

The Division of Extension was organized in 1909. In 1920 it became a bureau with Thomas Hall Shelby as director. Again, in 1924 it was changed to a division, and Shelby was made the first dean.

Note: After a considerable amount of reorganization, the division was changed into the College of Continuing Education in 1976, with Thomas Hatfield as dean.

Cass Gilbert had a heavy influence on the appearance of the campus. When he first visited at the request of the University's Regents in 1909, he found a motley collection of eight buildings of widely disparate styles and materials. Gilbert's acceptance of the invitation to design a new library in 1910 marked the beginning of an 11-year period during which he created, as University Architect, a style that remains pervasive. Battle Hall, the first separate library, set the general architectural style of the University as Spanish Renaissance and is still considered by many to be the architectural gem of the campus. The building was later used as the Barker Center to house the Texas History Collection; today it is part of the School of Architecture complex.

Sutton Hall, built in 1917, was also designed by Gilbert. It, too, is now used by the School of Architecture.

The Graduate Department (now School) was created by the Board of Regents in June 1910, in accordance with a plan recommended by the faculty on November 2, 1909. By the close of the 1910s major and minor work toward the degree of Master of Arts could be pursued in all schools of the College of Arts, with certain courses counted from the departments of Education and Engineering, with approval of the Graduate Council. Major work for the degree of Doctor of Philosophy was authorized in fourteen divisions. The first Ph.D. degree was conferred at the 1915 graduation exercises on Carl Gottfried Hartman. He was a member of the teaching staff of the Department of Zoology. The title of his dissertation was *Studies in the Development of the Opossum (Didelphys Virginiana): I. The History of the Early Cleavage. II. The Formation of the Blastocyst.*

The first woman to receive the Ph.D. degree at the University was Goldie Printis Horton in 1916. The title of her dissertation, in mathematics, was *Functions of Limited Variation and Lebesque Integrals.* She also taught at the University.

The College of Business Administration was first created as a department of the College of Arts in 1912. In

1922 it was made into a separate school, and in 1945 it was reorganized as a college. The degree of Bachelor of Business Administration was first offered in 1916.

Note: The entire complex of buildings that houses the College, including the Graduate School of Business Building and the University Teaching Center, is now called the George Kozmetsky Center for Business Education, named for a former dean and benefactor.

In 1913 the Athletic Council was organized. The new council was responsible to the faculty, the president of the University and the Board of Regents. L. Theo Bellmont was appointed director of athletics at the beginning of the 1913-1914 season. As a result of his initial efforts, the Southwest Intercollegiate Athletic Conference was organized on December 8, 1914. Eight universities, one of which was The University of Texas, became charter members. Others were Texas A&M, Oklahoma, Oklahoma A&M, Arkansas, Rice, Baylor, and Southwestern. The conference affiliated with the Cotton Bowl in 1940 and in 1942 ruled that SWC football champions must play in the Cotton Bowl.

In 1914 the name of the Alumni Association was changed to the "Ex-Students' Association of The University of Texas," and membership was broadened to include all former students.

Since the last quarter of the nineteenth century most colleges and universities have had mascots. Students at UT didn't actually get one that would become official until 1916. When Theo Bellmont came to the University in 1913 as director of athletics, he had an old mongrel dog the students named "Pig" for one of the football players. This dog played around the campus until he died in 1923. Students loved him and often referred to him as a mascot. When he died, they mourned at his funeral and buried him on the campus.

But on Thanksgiving Day, 1916, a Longhorn steer was presented to the students by a group of alumni from the Texas Panhandle. This first mascot was named "Bevo" (the name of a near-beer made in Austin by Anheuser-Busch). Later branded by the Aggies, he was barbecued and eaten at a banquet in 1920. Since that time, Texas has had a total of thirteen Bevos serve as mascots.

Note: Members of the Silver Spurs, an honor service organization, are Bevo's official custodians.

A blanket tax, or student activity fee, was adopted in the spring term of 1916. The tax was optional; but for $6.50, students were admitted to all athletic contests, glee club recitals, and band concerts, had subscriptions to the *Daily Texan* and *The University of Texas Magazine*, had use of the University boathouse, and also contributed to the support of the Students' Association, the Oratorical Association and certain other activities. The blanket tax put athletics on a better financial basis and resulted in larger attendance at games. The Students' Association had the responsibility of allocating the funds.

Note: The price of the blanket tax changed somewhat through the years, but it continued to be a bargain to students. In the 1970s the name was abolished, and the term "student fees" was adopted. Now all fees are not included in a "blanket tax."

Gov. James E. Ferguson launched an unexpected

attack on the University soon after his inauguration in January 1915. Sidney Mezes, who resigned in 1914 to become president of City College in New York, was replaced by Robert E. Vinson in 1916. (W. J. Battle served as *interim* president.) The governor called for the dismissal of Vinson, Battle, and several other faculty members in May 1917, saying he would veto the University's appropriation bill if his demands were not carried out. He also demanded abolition of all fraternities on the campus. Students and faculty protested and marched to the Capitol and down Congress Avenue on May 28, 1917. Outraged, Governor Ferguson vetoed the appropriation bill on June 2, 1917, but the attorney general declared the veto invalid because the governor had failed to veto the totals on the bill.

Will Hogg, a University graduate and generous benefactor, came to Austin and led the organization of a campaign to impeach the governor. The action culminated on September 22, 1917, when the Senate, sitting as a High Court of Impeachment, found the Governor guilty of the appropriation of State funds for his private use, the misapplication of funds, and the acceptance of large loans under questionable circumstances. He was removed from office.

During World War I (1917-1918), the School of Military Aeronautics, the Air School for Radio Operators, and the School of Auto Mechanics were established as subsidiaries of the University and operated until the armistice was signed. At the end of the war, on November 11, 1918, a ceremony was held on campus honoring 3,100 alumni in the service and eighty-five who had been killed in action.

About 1911 University officials began to construct wooden shacks for classrooms and laboratories, and during World War I their number was increased to accommodate the military training groups located on campus. This "Age of Shacks," or the period of "Shackeresque" architecture as it was called, began with a building for Domestic Economy in 1911 and ended with the tearing down of the same building in 1935. Two dozen unsightly wooden buildings, scattered across the campus, were used during this period. Students and faculty complained about them; they were cold in the winter, hot in the summer, and leaked when it rained. University President S.E. Mezes said that he wanted the shacks to be usable, but he wanted them to be so unsightly that Texans would become ashamed of them and somehow find money to replace them.

Note: These wooden shacks were the first ones. After World War II, another group of "temporary" buildings were moved to the campus.

During the administration of Gov. Pat Neff, a step of significance was taken toward the development of what was called the "Greater Campus." A campaign had been started to move the University campus to the Brackenridge Tract along the Colorado River. Col. George W. Brackenridge, a Regent, had given the University over four hundred acres of river front near the dam on the Colorado River. He wanted the campus moved to that site. A tremendous amount of opposition, including that of benefactor Maj. George W. Littlefield, developed. The forty-acre campus at that time was not sufficiently large enough to accommodate the rapidly growing student body following World War I.

Both houses of the legislature, after heated opposition, agreed upon an appropriation of $1.35 million for the purchase of additional acreage to the east of the

University. After deliberation and consultation with his friends and advisers, Governor Neff signed the bill on April 1, 1921. Whistles blew in Austin in approval, and both faculty and students at the University paraded to show their gratitude to Governor Neff.

The University acquired the land and buildings of the Blind Institute in 1925 (called "Little Campus" until renamed "Heman Sweatt Campus" in 1987, at IH-35 and Martin Luther King, Jr., Blvd.); the Cavanaugh homestead on Waller Creek in 1930; and in 1932 the property of old Texas Wesleyan College (between 24th and 26th streets and Waller Creek and Red River Street — present Law School site).

The fortieth anniversary of The University of Texas was celebrated on May 10, 11, and 13, 1923. The celebration officially opened on the afternoon of May 10, when Gov. Pat Neff, the first alumnus of the University to be elected governor of Texas, delivered the opening address. Dean T. U. Taylor and President Robert E. Vinson also spoke. That night Marie Taylor was crowned Queen of the University. Her coronation was followed by a reception and ball. The next afternoon the Varsity Circus opened with a street parade; that night, a historical pageant was presented at Clark Field. The final event, also on Clark Field, was a special performance of the Varsity Circus.

In 1923 oil was discovered in the middle of the two million acres of University lands in West Texas. The discovery well was Santa Rita #1. The University community rejoiced that it might now be possible to replace the unsightly wooden shacks on the campus.

Income from the state endowment constitutes the Permanent University Fund. Only income from this principal may be expended, not the direct revenues from the land or the principal itself. This earned income forms what is known as the Available University Fund. Because Texas A&M University was originally established as part of the University of Texas (the Academic and Law branches were in Austin and the Medical Branch was in Galveston), its System receives each year one-third of the Available Fund, except income from grazing leases. The remaining two-thirds goes to the University of Texas System.

Note: This agreement was negotiated in 1932 and the two universities became separate institutions. The Regents of the University of Texas were charged with management of the fund.

When Robert Vinson retired as president in 1923, William Seneca Sutton, dean of Education, was named to serve as *ad interim* president. Walter Marshall William Splawn, a member of the UT economics faculty and also a member of the Texas Railroad Commission, was elected president of UT in 1924. While president he lent his expertise to the investment of funds from the recent finding of oil on UT lands in West Texas and fostered development of the graduate school. He resigned in 1927.

The story of the construction of Memorial Stadium in 1924 is a dramatic record of Texas loyalty. L. Theo Bellmont started the drive and was the guiding force in bringing it to a successful completion. Under the leadership of William McGill and sixty-eight captains, five hundred student workers raised pledges of $150,000 for the fund in a six-day campus drive; this amount was increased to $165,000 by H. Lutcher Stark, a member of the Board of Regents. Students fired a cannon as each

$10,000 mark was passed. Citizens of Austin raised another $150,000 in pledges in another short campaign, and alumni and other friends in the state added another $150,000. At the dedication of Memorial Stadium on Thanksgiving Day that same year, twenty-seven special trains brought visitors from all parts of the state to hear ex-governor Pat Neff make the dedicatory address and to see Texas defeat Texas A&M, 7-0. (Baylor had defeated Texas 28–10 two weeks earlier in the first game played in the stadium.)

The School of Pharmacy moved from Galveston to the Main University campus in 1927. It was first established at the Medical Branch in 1893. When it came to Austin its name was changed to the College of Pharmacy, and W. F. Gidley was appointed the first dean.

Note: Graduate programs in pharmacy were added during the administration of Henry M. Burlage, who was dean from 1947 to 1962.

In 1929 the University was selected as a member of the Association of American Universities. Even today it is one of only three Southwestern members of the AAU, which is composed of the fifty-eight leading universities in the United States and Canada.

Dr. W. J. Battle, chairman of the building committee during this significant period, wrote: "In 1930, the Texas Legislature proposed, and the people adopted, a constitutional amendment permitting Regents to borrow money from the Permanent Fund to erect the necessary buildings. The sum of $4,000,000 was agreed upon. In 1932, the

Legislature passed an enabling act approving the financial program."

The building committee decided to construct first the following buildings: Library (now back part of Main), Physics (Painter Hall), Home Economics (Gearing Hall), Geology (Hogg Building), Engineering (Taylor Hall), Architecture (Goldsmith Hall), Auditorium (Hogg), Men's Dormitory (Brackenridge Hall), and a student's union (Texas Union). To these were added a new practice school for teaching (University Junior High School; now Education Annex), additional dormitories (Andrews, Carothers, Roberts, and Prather), and most important of all — the Main Building and Tower. The Regents employed Paul P. Cret of Philadelphia as consulting architect. Greene, LaRoche, and Dahl were the architects, and supervising architect and architect for the Texas Union and Auditorium was J. M. White. At Round-Up time in 1933, nine of the new buildings were dedicated. A new era for the University had begun.

Cret, the consulting architect for these and other buildings constructed from 1930 until 1945, exerted a tremendous influence on the University. His 1933 plan for the UT campus is a masterpiece of understanding and foresight. He accepted Gilbert's ideas as essentially sound, but Cret's work had a unique character that gave the campus a treasured identity.

As early as 1907 the Ex-Students' Association selected Thomas Watt Gregory to be chairman of a committee to provide a new gymnasium. Approximately $65,000 was collected and invested at the time. Gregory left for Washington to be active in the Woodrow Wilson administration and didn't return to Austin until 1927. Elected president of the

Ex-Students' Association, he proposed to the University Regents that the original plan be extended to include a women's gymnasium (now Hiss) and a student union building (now Texas Union). The response was spontaneous and enthusiastic. Students participated in the drive for funds and recorded the results of their work on a huge thermometer at the west entrance to Old Main. The entire project was accomplished. An auditorium (Hogg) was constructed as a separate building. Originally, it was planned as a part of the Texas Union.

Littlefield Memorial Fountain was turned on for the first time on March 26, 1932. It was part of the Littlefield Memorial Entrance Gate, a gift of Maj. George Littlefield. Designed by Pompeii Coppini, it was arranged in place by consulting architect Paul P. Cret. The memorial included all of the statues on the Main Mall except the one of George Washington. They were not placed as Coppini had planned; as a result, he claimed that the concept was changed.

The statue of George Washington, completed later, was requested and financed by the Daughters of the American Revolution. Coppini's last, it was at one time the only statue of Washington west of the Mississippi River.

The building program was the happy climax in the long story of the University's physical expansion. The growth was the expression in stone and steel of the loyalty and undying spirit of those who had high hopes for a great university — a "university of the first class." Dedicated alumni felt a symbolic meaning in the razing of the north wing of Old Main in 1932, even though it housed the old auditorium that had been condemned and unused since 1915. "Brick can be pulled from brick to make way for material progress," one wrote, "but the essential significance of the Main building can never be destroyed or diminished. It is itself a corner stone."

The present Main Building, with its Tower, was completed in 1937. Designed by Cret, it was built of Bedford, Indiana, limestone; its style, like so many other buildings of its period, is modified Spanish Renaissance.

Seventeen bells (not a complete carillon) originally hung in the Tower. In 1987, thirty-nine new bells were added to make the fifty-six-bell carillon the largest in Texas and one of the largest in the country. Named the Knicker Carillon (for Hedway Thusmelda Knicker, the benefactor), the bells were dedicated on November 14, 1987.

Through the years the Tower has come to have different meanings to people. Its orange top is a symbol of victory (nothing is darker than that Tower after an athletic defeat); it also honors special academic achievements, and as a group, special University benefactors. The entire shaft becomes orange as graduates receive degrees. To alumni everywhere, it has a personal significance. It symbolizes the University.

Plan II, a course of study leading to the B.A. degree that permitted students to take cultural rather than professional courses, went into effect in 1935, when one hundred freshmen were accepted in the pilot program. Dean H. T. Parlin developed the idea; he received assistance from some of the young, enthusiastic professors in the College of Arts and Sciences. Plan II, which celebrated its 60th anniversary in 1995, is one of the oldest honors programs in the country.

Texas Memorial Museum was built on the UT campus in 1937 in honor of the Texas Centennial. Paul Cret was consulting architect. Ground was broken for the building by President Franklin D. Roosevelt in 1936 during a whistle stop in Austin. In 1959 ownership was passed from the state to the University, where it is dedicated to the study and interpretation of the natural and social sciences, with emphasis on Texas, the Southwest, and Latin America.

Note: The statue "Mustangs" in front of the museum is the work of Alexander Phimister Proctor and was a gift of Ralph Ogden; it was dedicated in 1948.

Harry Yandell Benedict, tenth president of the University, died on May 10, 1937. He graduated from the University in 1892, completed graduate work at Harvard, and joined the UT faculty in 1899 as a teacher of mathematics and astronomy. He served as University president from 1927 until his death. Fifteen buildings were constructed on campus during his administration. His influence on the development of the University was of lasting significance.

Following President Benedict's death, John William Calhoun, University comptroller, was appointed president *ad interim*. He served until 1939.

Homer Price Rainey, a native Texan, received his graduate degrees from the University of Chicago and came from Bucknell University to become president of the University of Texas in 1939. He was the first UT president to be nominated by a faculty committee. He was also the first to be fired by the Board of Regents (November 1, 1944) by a 6-2 vote during a dispute about academic freedom.

Both faculty and students protested his firing and

marched to the Capitol to request Gov. Coke Stevenson to invite the Regents to meet with them. They didn't. Students and faculty adopted a resolution asking for Rainey's reinstatement. They didn't get it. During the controversy the University was placed on probation by the Southern Association of Colleges and Schools and was censured by the American Association of University Professors.

Theophilus Shickel Painter served as acting president from 1944 until 1946 and then as president until 1952. He was a professor of zoology.

The Bible years were important in the development of the Athletic Department at the University. Dana Xenophon Bible, son of a college professor, brought an articulation to his profession that gained him wide respect as a speaker and writer. He came to Texas as football coach and athletic director in the fall of 1937 under a contract that was unusual in those Depression years. The contract was for ten years at $15,000 per year, about twice the amount the president of the University was making and nearly four times the salary of the Texas governor. He remained at Texas as coach until the end of the 1946 season; then he continued as athletic director for another ten years.

His 1940 team was pictured on the cover of *Life*, marking the first time that magazine had ever shown the entire starting football team individually. On the following Saturday, Baylor tied Texas, 7-7, and TCU later beat Texas, 14-7, knocking the Longhorns from its rank as #1 in the nation.

The College of Fine Arts was organized in 1938. E. William Doty served as dean from its founding until his retirement in 1971. Composed of the departments of Art,

Drama and Music, its first faculty numbered ten members. They taught the one hundred and forty fine arts students in what is now Battle Hall.

Note: Today's facilities on the east side of the campus are among the finest in the nation.

The Hogg Foundation for Mental Health was established on the campus of the University in September 1940. It was made possible by the children of Governor James S. Hogg, who wanted it to serve the people of Texas. Its initial endowment came primarily from the estate of Will C. Hogg, whose sister, Ima Hogg, and brothers, Thomas E. Hogg and Mike Hogg, and their widows played a major role in establishing the foundation under the University's Board of Regents. Dr. Robert L. Sutherland was its first director.

Note: In 1995 the Hogg Foundation offices were moved from the main campus to larger quarters on the Brackenridge Tract on Lake Austin Boulevard. The director reports to the UT Austin president.

The Institute of Latin American Studies was formally established in 1941. Its purpose was to coordinate an extensive instructional program dealing with Latin American civilization and development at undergraduate and graduate levels and support research by faculty and graduate students on various Latin American topics.

Note: The Institute is the oldest and largest of the interdisciplinary programs on the UT campus. It is currently located in Sid Richardson Hall, adjacent to the Nettie Lee Benson Latin American Collection.

The World War II years brought a new look to the UT

campus. Several naval groups were trained at the University. A large number of men and a few women entered the service, and other UT women took a special war-conditioning course, did volunteer work with the Red Cross and other groups, and became accustomed to wartime rationing. Women students, for the first time, served as student body president and editor of the *Daily Texan.*

When the war ended on V-J Day in 1945, students joined the big celebration. Using the G.I. Bill, numerous students enrolled in the University in the years immediately following the war. A severe housing shortage and the need for more classroom space resulted in immediate plans for additional campus construction.

After the war ended, barracks that originally housed workers who built B-24 bombers were given to the University to house ex-G.I.'s and were shipped from Wichita, Kansas to Austin by freight cars in 1947. They were the original Brackenridge Apartments, replaced in 1980-1982, on Lake Austin Boulevard.

Despite the critical wartime shortages during the early 1940s, the Music Building (now Rainey Hall), with its Jessen Auditorium and Aeolian-Skinner pipe organ, and the Chemical Engineering (now E. P. Schoch) and Petroleum Engineering (now Economics) buildings were completed (1942).

After the war the University entered Shack Era II or the "Age of G.I. Halls," when fourteen new temporary buildings were moved to the campus in 1947 from Camp Wallace, near Galveston, as part of a Federal Works Administration project. The buildings housed thirty-six classrooms, four chemistry laboratories, a Health Service annex, a cafeteria, an engineering workshop, faculty offices, and the Veterans' Administration on-campus office. Students hated them. The last one, called CP Hall, was razed as the Nursing Building was completed in 1973.

An all-male Faculty Council was organized in 1945. The faculty organization has changed from time to time in an effort to give the faculty more voice in planning the academic procedures for the University.

Heman Marion Sweatt, an African-American, was denied entry to UT's Law School in 1946, but after a four-year court battle he was admitted in September 1950. Eight other African-Americans preceded him as graduate students in the University by being admitted to summer terms. Before this incident, the majority of students at The University of Texas had been European-Americans. The number of students from Mexico and South American countries had been minimal.

The Graduate School of Library Science was established in 1948, with Robert Raymond Douglas as director. The title was changed to dean in the early 1970s.

The Graduate School of Social Work was organized in 1950, with Lora Lee Pederson as director. The title of the administrator for this area was also changed to dean in 1972.

James Pinckney Hart was the first chancellor of the University of Texas. He occupied the position from the time it was created in 1950 until his resignation on December 31, 1953. Logan Wilson, the new president, was also named acting chancellor. The University's chancellor has responsibility for the entire University System, which at that time included only the Medical Branch at Galveston, the College of Mines and Metallurgy (now UT El Paso), the M. D. Anderson Cancer Center in Houston, the Dental Branch in Houston, and Southwestern Medical School in Dallas. Between September 30, 1954, and September 1960, the title was abolished, but it was then recreated with Logan Wilson as chancellor.

The System offices were on the Main Campus until 1970, when they were moved to West Sixth Street in downtown Austin.

During the 1950s a construction boom provided more than twenty new buildings on the campus at a total cost of more than $20 million. Student enrollment, which had been about seven thousand at the end of the war, reached eighteen thousand in 1960. The new buildings provided classroom and residence hall accommodations as well as service facilities.

The buildings completed in the 1950s were the Student Health Center, Experimental Science Building, six women's cooperatives, Pharmacy Building, Batts, Mezes, Benedict, and Parlin halls, Journalism Building (now Geography), Service Building, the new Law facility, Simkins Hall, Blanton, and Kinsolving dormitories, Moore Hall and Varsity Center, Russell Steindam Hall and Rifle Range, and the W. R. Woolrich Laboratories.

Completely air-conditioned when it was built, the $4,272,000 Experimental Science Building was finished in 1951. It was one of the largest facilities in the United States dedicated to scientific research at the time.

After World War II the architects tended to move away from the original red tile roofs of the Cret era. Architecture began to be more eclectic. Accommodation of the University's increasing enrollment was the rule.

Mark Lemon of Dallas was consulting architect for most, but not all, of the new construction during the 1950s.

Note: The new construction and renovation of the 1950s was a major turning point in the development of the University. The air-conditioned buildings made possible a year-round calendar, heretofore infeasible in the hot Texas summers.

The University, under a dollar-a-year lease agreement with the War Assets Administration in 1946, acquired the multi-million dollar magnesium plant eight miles northwest of the campus, which subsequently became the Balcones Research Center (now the J. J. Pickle Research Campus). Use of the plant for research at the time released valuable space on campus for teaching.

The 1950s was a time of quiet rebuilding after the tumultuous years following the firing of President Rainey. President Logan Wilson laid to rest much of the bitterness that had developed and avoided confrontation with warring factions that still debated the issues of the Rainey administration. Faculty salaries rose and academic standards improved. Dr. Wilson and Dr. Harry Ransom broke the custom of using monies from the Available Fund for building construction only. They pleaded for "more brains, less bricks," and asked for one million to be used as an "Excellence Fund." The Regents granted their request.

The Board of Regents, in July 1955, decreed complete racial desegregation beginning in 1956-1957, and the immediate desegregation of the Main University graduate school. Few African-Americans enrolled, however, because housing was still segregated, as were most facilities in the University area.

In the spring of 1957 Barbara Smith (now Conrad), a young African-American woman student, was cast in the lead role of a University production of *Dido and Aeneas*, opposite a European-American male. Publicity, controversy, and pressure followed, and Barbara was removed from the part on orders from the president's office. Her removal caused further criticism of the University, but Barbara was applauded two decades later for her performance as Marian Anderson in ABC's mini-series, "Franklin and Eleanor." In 1985 she was chosen as a Distinguished Alumna of the University. She currently sings with the Metropolitan Opera.

Darrell Royal, a former all-American football player at the University of Oklahoma, started an era of championship football at UT, when he arrived in 1957. When he retired as coach after twenty years, he was a national coaching legend, with a winning percentage of .778, three national championships, eleven Southwest Conference championships, and sixteen bowl games.

Note: Royal resigned as coach following the December 4, 1976, victory over Arkansas. He continued to serve as athletic director until January 1, 1980, when he became special assistant to the president for athletic programs, the first such position in the country.

The University officially celebrated its seventy-fifth anniversary at a convocation of faculty, staff, laypersons, students, and distinguished educators from other colleges and universities in 1958. President Logan Wilson and Gov. Price Daniel cut the ribbons to open the celebration. The year-long work of the Committee of 75, with Rex G. Baker, Sr., as chairman, and the Conference on Expectations provided a blueprint for the future. Among numerous recommendations, a greater emphasis on the development of the University's graduate programs and research received special attention.

Note: When the University celebrated its 100th anniversary twenty-five years later, the chairman of that Commission, Wales H. Madden, Jr., remarked, "The wisdom and foresight of that Committee and the soundness of the direction it afforded the University have met the critical scrutiny of time. Many believe it is due to the Committee of 75's vision that The University has enjoyed the past highly successful twenty-five years."

In 1958 the University established the Computation Center in the Experimental Science Building with an IBM 650 computer, a small staff, and a vision of the usefulness of such a facility. In 1961 the Center moved to the new Computation Center. Through the years the system has been updated several times.

Note: Today (1997) central academic computing facilities are available to all academic departments and research centers, and to students, faculty members, and staff members. The Center operates two super-computers, many smaller, specialized computer servers and time-sharing systems, and a two hundred-seat Student Microcomputer Facility in the Flawn Academic Center. The System is very complex in order to be usable and of service to all who need it.

The Computation Center's High Performance Computing Facility (HPCF) serves the research and instructional super-computing needs of the University and of other Texas institutions of higher education. Located at the J. J. Pickle Research Campus, the HPCF is accessible to the University community via UTnet.

Today every University student currently enrolled

either owns a computer or has free and convenient access to one on campus. UT Austin recently joined with other major US research universities to participate in the creation of a new national network to be called Internet2, which will offer vastly higher connection speeds and more reliable services. It will allow the simultaneous transmission of voice, video, and data to enable distance learning, embrace digital libraries and make possible new realms of on-line collaborative research.

In 1958 the Ex-Students' Association and the University began the practice of formally honoring former University students who have been recognized in their professions, and by their communities, as outstanding citizens. Since that time, honorees have been presented at a Distinguished Awards gala.

Harry H. Ransom was named chancellor on April 1, 1961. In 1963 the presidency as a separate office was abolished, and Ransom served in the dual position of chancellor and president until 1967, when Ransom resigned and the presidency was re-established, with Norman Hackerman as president. Ransom resigned as chancellor on December 31, 1970, and was named chancellor *emeritus*, a position he retained until his death in April 1976. His tenure was one of the longest in UT history. While he was chief administrator, the University was hailed as a "Cambridge on the Range," and its library was one of five in the United States included in Anthony Hobson's *Great Libraries* (1970).

Hackerman came to the University as assistant professor of chemistry in 1945 and was promoted to full professor in 1950. He served as vice president and provost from 1961 to 1963 and president from 1967 until 1970, when he resigned to become president of Rice University.

Even though architectural education began at UT in 1910 when Dean T. U. Taylor of engineering asked Hugo F. Kuehne to start a school of architecture, not until 1965 was a separate school of architecture organized. Philip Douglas Creer was the first director. Alan Y. Taniguchi was the first dean (1969-1972).

The University's enrollment jumped from approximately twenty thousand in 1960 to more than thirty-five thousand in 1969. To accommodate this increasing enrollment, a Master Plan Development Report plotted an expanding campus, and new buildings of the 1960s included the Computation Center, West Mall Office Building, Business-Economics Building, Drama (Winship) Building, Undergraduate Library (Flawn), Art Building, Engineering-Science Building, Alumni Center, Calhoun Hall, Geology Building, East Wing of Townes Hall, Patterson Laboratory, Jester Center, and Music Building East (new band hall).

The Beauford H. Jester Center, which accommodates over three thousand men and women students, opened in September 1969. This facility doubled the amount of residence hall space just as many students were enjoying their newfound freedom by choosing apartment living, made more convenient by the shuttle bus system that was begun by the Students' Association a few years earlier. The Center also had classrooms, an auditorium, departmental offices, service centers, and a store. It was the University's first experiment in co-educational living.

During the 1960s racial integration took steps forward. The Longhorn Band had its first African-American member in 1962, and the first black was elected to the Students' Assembly in the same year. Darrell Royal announced that football was integrated in 1963, but the first black to receive a scholarship was Leon O'Neal in 1968. Julius Whittier was the first African-American to letter at UT (1970), and Roosevelt Leaks was the first to become a star (1971-1973). The Interfraternity Council announced that it was no longer segregated in the spring of 1964, and in 1965 the Texas Cowboys no longer staged a black-faced minstrel as they had since they were organized in 1922.

In May 1964 the Regents removed all racial barriers at UT, including those affecting housing. Dr. Ervin S. Perry, for whom the Perry-Castaneda Library is named, was the first African-American professor. He was employed as a professor of engineering in May 1964. Cora Eiland Hicks was a teaching assistant in the English Department prior to Perry, but Perry was actually the first black professor.

The faculty of the 1960s was a representation of both old and new Texas. Harry Ransom started a kind of inner brain trust of younger, well-educated men that many referred to as "Harry's boys." He was also interested in creating an excellent library. He planned and had built the Academic Center (now the Peter T. Flawn Academic Center), an open-shelf library for undergraduates. Furthermore, he began assembling one of the finest collections of twentieth century literature in existence. By the end of the 1960s, several programs at the University were ranked among the best in the country, and UT was becoming a major research university.

Two tragic events occurred on the campus from the Main Building Tower in the mid-1960s. On August 10, 1965, a fire in the Tower apparently started from sparks of molten metal from cutting tools used by workers installing an air conditioning system in the building. The Tower's basic structure was not affected, but considerable damage was done. Near the flames were some of the University's valuable collections.

Note: Since that time, steps have been taken to deposit all valuable collections in more secure, fireproof, climate-controlled facilities.

A catastrophic event occurred on August 1, 1966. A twenty-five-year-old student, Charles Joseph Whitman, climbed to the top of the Tower and began firing a high-powered rifle at students and passersby on and near the campus. Before he stopped, he took the lives of sixteen people and injured thirty-one others. The night before, he had killed his wife and mother, according to a note he left, to protect them from embarrassment. An officer killed Whitman in a dramatic encounter on the Tower parapet ninety minutes after the shooting began. An autopsy revealed a brain tumor, which had caused him to suffer severe headaches.

Note: After this event, the University administration took steps to improve counseling for students. The Twenty-four Hour Counseling and Referral Service was established in 1967 and is still in operation. The Tower has been closed to visitors since 1974. It has been the site if nine deaths. The last suicide occurred on November 28, 1974.

The School of Communication was organized in 1966, bringing together speech, journalism, advertising, and radio-television-film. DeWitt C. Reddick was the first dean. A department (called School at the time) of

Journalism was first organized in 1914.

Note: Since 1978 the Jesse H. Jones Communication Center has housed the School and Texas Student Publications, including the Daily Texan *and the* Cactus.

The Lyndon B. Johnson School of Public Affairs admitted its first students in 1970 in the new Sid Richardson Hall. The first dean was John A. Gronouski, former Postmaster General of the United States (1963-1965) and ambassador to Poland (1965-1968). He served as dean from 1970 to 1973.

Frank C. Erwin, Jr., was a Regent of the University from 1963 until 1975, and served as chairman from 1966 until 1971. His tenure was marked by the student protests of the late 1960s and early 1970s, the division of the College of Arts and Sciences, and a rapid increase in enrollment. Under his tenure, The University of Texas System was expanded and reorganized. Erwin was not a Regent who stood back and observed; he was an active participant in the activities of the University.

When students caused a construction halt near Waller Creek after Erwin had ordered the removal of some large trees to prepare for the expansion of Memorial Stadium, he ordered their arrest so that work might proceed.

Erwin's aggressiveness was often criticized, but his devotion to the University and his ability to work well with the legislature made him a great asset for UT.

In 1967 when Erwin was chairman of the Board of Regents, the sixtieth legislature changed the names of all the component institutions in the UT System to indicate the institution and its location. The University of Texas became "The University of Texas at Austin." At that time, the system was made up of only eight components, but in 1969, the sixty-first legislature authorized six others.

Note: Other changes have occurred in the System since 1969, but the chancellor is the presiding officer over these components; each separate institution has a president.

The University Council was formed in 1969 and continued to function as the chief legislative/discussion arm of the faculty and administration until 1995. It consisted of approximately twenty-five administrative members *ex officio* with vote and two or three (varying) without vote, fifty-three voting members of the General Faculty, and six students with vote. The president presided at council meetings, and the secretary of the General Faculty served as *ex officio* secretary of the council. It initiated legislation, acted on recommendations, and conducted studies and investigations. The faculty members of the council formed the Faculty Senate, a "separate forum for free discussion and decision regarding a broad range of matters of importance to the University . . . ."

Note: In 1995 the Senate and University Council were both abolished when a new organization, called the Faculty Council, was created.

During the 1969-1970 session, a severe internal University crisis occurred. The issues involved the relations among the Regents, the president, and the dean of arts and sciences, John Silber. The primary question was whether the College of Arts and Sciences should be split, a matter that sharply divided students, faculty, and regents. Dean Silber opposed and spoke out against the division and was dismissed in July 1970. Students protested loudly. Dr. Bryce Jordan was acting president, a position to which he was appointed after Dr. Hackerman resigned in 1970; Dr. Charles LeMaister was chancellor, a position he had held since Dr. Ransom had resigned on January 1, 1970. Frank Erwin was chairman of the Regents.

In 1970 the College of Arts and Sciences was divided into three colleges and a division. The first deans for the divided College were Samuel P. Ellison, Jr., College of Natural Sciences; James W. McKie, College of Social and Behavioral Sciences; Stanley N. Werbow, College of Humanities; and James R. Roach, Division of General and Comparative Studies. Stanley R. Ross was appointed provost for the Arts and Sciences in 1973.

Note: In 1978, on recommendation of President Lorene Rogers, the Board of Regents reunited the College of Humanities and Social and Behavioral Sciences and the Division of General and Comparative Studies into a new College of Liberal Arts, with Robert D. King as dean.

In September 1970 the administrative offices of the University of Texas System were moved from the UT campus to the Claudia Taylor Johnson Complex on West 6th Street in downtown Austin. The complex eventually consisted of three buildings: Claudia Taylor Johnson Hall, formerly the US Post Office; O. Henry Hall, also formerly a US Post Office and Federal Courthouse; and Ashbel Smith Hall, a building constructed between 1972 and 1975.

Note: In 1991 the University System purchased the Colorado Building near the complex.

Dr. Jim Ayres of the Department of English at UT began his work at Winedale with a semester class of fourteen students on November 15, 1970, on receiving an invitation from Miss Ima Hogg to perform in the Winedale Theatre Barn at Round Top, Texas. Since that time, Ayres and his students have performed twenty-three of Shakespeare's thirty-seven plays, repeating some of them several times.

Note: Shakespeare at Winedale celebratèd its twenty-fifth anniversary in August 1996. The program is nationally recognized as an innovative approach to Shakespeare.

The Vietnam War and the nationwide student protests brought sweeping changes in University policies, enrollment, and standards. Students for a Democratic Society, a New Left organization of national scope, had a small but active chapter at UT. Protests on campus were common during the last half of the 1960s and the first half of the 1970s. Stump speaking provided one way for students to vent their emotions.

When the United States marched into Cambodia in 1970 and the Kent State University shootings occurred, students at UT gathered by the thousands on the Main Mall to protest. On Friday, May 8, 1970, an estimated twenty thousand marched downtown in peaceful protest of the War, U.S. involvement in Cambodia, and the four Kent State deaths.

The first Presidential Library on a university campus was dedicated on the campus of the University of Texas on May 22, 1971, when some four thousand friends, followers, and members of the University community gathered for the dedication of the Lyndon Baines Johnson Library. Nothing dampened the jovial mood of the crowd, not even the muggy weather, the long lines at the barbecue buffet, the strict security, the chants of "no more war" from demonstrators a few blocks away, or the black balloons rising in protest of the Vietnam War. Regents Chairman Frank C. Erwin, Jr., presided at the ceremony. President Richard Nixon officially accepted the library for the federal government; Reverend Billy Graham delivered the invocation, and former President and Mrs. Lyndon Johnson enjoyed the special occasion.

Dr. Stephen H. Spurr, graduate dean at the University of Michigan, was appointed president of UT Austin in 1971 after a faculty-student committee conducted a nationwide search. He came into conflict with Chancellor Charles LeMaister and the Regents over several issues never publicly explained. In September 1974, when President Spurr refused to resign, Chancellor LeMaister fired him. The Board of Regents, with John Peace as chairman, in a divided vote, confirmed his firing. Many students and faculty members questioned the action. Dr. Spurr continued his University relationship as a professor in the Lyndon B. Johnson School of Public Affairs.

Vice President Lorene Rogers was appointed Acting President upon the dismissal of President Stephen H. Spurr. Almost a year later, on September 12, 1975, she was named president, the first woman president of a major university. The faculty-student advisory committee had recommended against her appointment, but the Board of Regents, in a divided vote, accepted Chancellor LeMaister's recommendation that she be made president.

Approximately six thousand students crowded onto the Main Mall in the September noon heat shouting for her resignation. Another large group later marched to the homes of Regents chairman Allan Shivers, Chancellor Charles LeMaister, Regent Frank Erwin, Jr., and President Rogers. The General Faculty adopted a resolution requesting faculty members to refuse to serve on standing committees President Rogers appointed, or to take part in University Council proceedings. The boycott lasted a year.

During the 1970s the University continued to expand to accommodate the growing student body. The 262 acres making up the contiguous campus in 1970 was increased to 316 acres by 1979. Building construction slowed down by the end of the decade but not before fifteen new buildings had been added and several others enlarged or renovated. Included among the new ones were the Harry Ransom Center, to house the ever-growing Humanities Research Collection, R. L. Moore and Ernest Cockrell halls, the Jesse H. Jones Communication Complex, the Perry-Castaneda Library, the Nursing Building, the College of Education Building (now Sanchez Hall), and some of the finest facilities for athletics in the country: Disch-Falk Field, Frank C. Erwin Special Events Center, and Lee and Joe Jamail Texas Swimming Center.

The School of Nursing was moved from Galveston to become a part of UT Austin in 1976. Originally an integral part of the Medical Branch, a System-wide School of Nursing was established in 1967 to meet the need for more nurses. The School had six branches, including one in Austin. In 1976 the System organization was dissolved, and the Austin branch, with Billye Brown as dean, became a part of UT Austin.

The Perry-Castaneda Library, opened at the beginning of the fall 1977 semester and now serves as the main library of the University, replacing the library in the Main

Building (1934-1977). The new facility was named for Dr. Ervin Perry, the University's first African-American professor, and Dr. Carlos Eduardo Castaneda, professor of Latin American history and Latin American Collection librarian. The building, dedicated on November 17, 1977, has 500,673 square feet of floor space and has book stacks open to all. The card catalogue is computerized and may be accessed at the many terminals on the campus.

Note: The University's library possibly existed when the University was in the Temporary Capitol in the fall of 1883. Former librarian and historian E. W. Winkler wrote that it had fewer than one thousand volumes at the time, and J. E. Goodwin, also a former librarian, noted that its first recorded home was in the state (Temporary) Capitol, but no documentation is available that establishes its location or confirms its actual existence as a service unit. Thirty years later M. W. Humphreys, a member of the original faculty, stated that the library was not available for students or faculty until after the University had moved to the completed West Wing of the Main Building early in 1884. During the first years of operation female students and faculty had full access to the collection, but books for male students were paged by the librarian.

From these meager beginnings, the various libraries of The University of Texas at Austin now constitute the fifth-largest academic library in the United States, with approximately seven million volumes. It includes the General Libraries, the Tarlton Law Library, and the Humanities Research Center.

The first Heman Sweatt Symposium was held in the spring of 1987. Named for the man whose law suit resulted in the admission of African-Americans to UT (1950), the early symposia focused on civil rights in the United States. As it developed, it focused on broader issues of the African and African American struggle for freedom and equality around the world.

Peter Tyrrell Flawn, an internationally known geologist who had been a long-time member of the UT Austin faculty and president of UT San Antonio, was named president of UT Austin on September 1, 1979. A Yale University graduate, he began his administration with vigor, pledging a "War on Mediocrity." He served as president for six years. Major highlights of his administration were the celebration of the University's 100th anniversary in 1983, an extensive building program, a new core curriculum, a larger number of Merit Scholars than any other public university, and the matching-funds endowment program for faculty positions.

His administration saw the completion of the College of Fine Arts Performing Arts Center, which includes Bass Concert Hall, Drama Workshops, Music Building and Bates Recital Hall, McCullough Theatre, and Fine Arts Library and Administration Building.

Note: Other buildings in the Fine Arts Complex, completed earlier, are the Art Building and Museum and Music Building East.

Among other buildings completed during the Flawn administration were the Engineering Teaching Center II, the Townes Hall Annex and the University Teaching Center.

President Flawn also took steps to improve teaching, recruit more minorities, tighten admission standards, and enhance the quality of life on campus.

UT's first endowed faculty position was created in 1959. Flawn established the Centennial Endowment Program in 1980, with the University matching gifts for endowed chairs. At the time, UT had a total of 110 endowed positions. As the University began its 101st year, the number of endowed positions was 802.

Note: Today (1997) they number more than 1,100.

In March 1980 the United States Department of Energy chose the University as the site for the new national Institute for Fusion Studies, which would bring together the world's foremost physicists and energy researchers. The new Texas Experimental Tokamak (TEXT) was dedicated in May 1981.

Also of significance in the area of academic development in the early 1980s was the probing of Gulf of Mexico waters by University marine biologists at the Marine Science Institute on the Gulf Coast, and the sending of laser beams to the moon by the University scientists at the McDonald Observatory in the Davis Mountains of West Texas.

Note: Currently (1997), eighty-seven organized research units are a part of UT Austin. Research is funded by grants and contracts from governmental agencies, and from the private sector, through gifts from individuals, foundations and corporations, from the Available University Fund, and through state appropriations.

The Retired Faculty-Staff Association was organized in the spring of 1982 to provide opportunities for UT retired persons to remain more closely associated with University life. The University provided a staff liaison to work with the organization. The first president of RFSA was Nevada Blackburn.

Note: Since it was organized, RFSA, over five hundred members, has established a scholarship endowment fund that currently has in it over $100,000.

The calendar year of 1983 was designated the official

Centennial year for The University of Texas at Austin, and included major Centennial programs and activities. The Centennial Program Office, over which Shirley Bird Perry presided as director, coordinated all Centennial activities; Susan Clagett held primary responsibilities for the programmatic aspects of the entire Centennial program.

A Centennial Commission of approximately one hundred seventy-five distinguished individuals (of whom thirty-five were honorary) representing a cross-section of the citizens of Texas and the University's alumni was appointed, with Wales H. Madden, Jr., as chairman. The Commission was charged with an assessment of the current condition of the University and with making recommendations regarding future priorities and directions for the institution. The report of the Commission was made public on September 15, 1983.

Special celebrations included, among others, Opening Day Activities, Student Leader Reunion, Centennial Honors Day, Centennial Commencement, Opening of Centennial Exhibit at the LBJ Library, Centennial Anniversary Convocation, Centennial Showcase/Exposition, and Closing Day Activities.

The renovation of two Little Campus buildings at the corner of Martin Luther King, Jr., Boulevard and IH 35 accomplished a note of nostalgia. The Nowotny Building, first built in 1862, once housed Gen. George Custer. The other building, now Hargis Hall, was first constructed as a boys' dormitory in the Blind Asylum. Both buildings had been used for numerous purposes.

In August 1987 the portion of the campus known as "Little Campus" was renamed the "Heman Sweatt Campus" in memory of one of the first African-Americans to enroll at the University.

During the University's centennial celebration (1983), the Friar Society established a prestigious teaching fellowship, with an annual prize that carried a $10,000 stipend. A number of faculty awards are given each year, but the Friar's award remains the largest. Award nominees are carefully considered from a list of nominees, and during the selection process members of the organization attend classes of nominees and consider student evaluations and other pertinent data.

Note: The Friar Society was established in 1911, and has been considered one of the highest student honor societies on campus. Formerly all-male, it became co-ed in the early 1970s.

University President Peter Flawn announced on October 12, 1984, that James Michener had established a permanent affiliation with the University. He came to Austin in October 1982 to work on a major novel about Texas, which was published in 1986, the Texas Sesquicentennial.

In 1989 Michener and his wife, Mari, gave the University $3 million to establish the Texas Center for Writers. The stated purpose of the program was to provide for creative writers across the disciplinary lines of English, theatre and dance, and radio-television-film.

Since the original gift, the Micheners have donated $15 million to fund an interdisciplinary Master of Fine Arts in Writing, which was approved in the summer of 1992. Both graduate and post-graduate students may hold the Michener Fellowships in the program.

The Micheners also gave a large collection of twentieth century American art (375 paintings) to the University. It is currently housed in the Archer M. Huntington Art Gallery in the Harry Ransom Humanities Research Center.

Note: In February 1997 the University announced that

it would soon have a new art museum named for Jack Blanton of Houston. Houston Endowment pledged $12 million in his honor toward its construction. Other major donors are James Michener and Bernard Rapoport.

After President Flawn resigned in 1985 to pursue other interests, Dr. William H. Cunningham, who had been dean of the College of Business Administration and the Graduate School of Business since 1983, was named president. Dr. Gerard Fonken, who had been vice president for academic affairs and research under Flawn, was appointed to the new position of executive vice president and provost.

Cunningham first came to the University in 1971 as an assistant professor of marketing. Fonken came in 1959 as a research scientist and instructor of chemistry.

In 1986 the Ex-Students' Association celebrated its one hundredth anniversary. At commencement that year four prominent alumni were speakers, and one hundred other alumni were invited to march in the evening processional to represent over 300,000 [now 375,000] alumni all over the world.

Started in the early 1970s, Services for Students with Disabilities in the Dean of Students Office, removed many barriers faced by disabled UT students. In 1989 a full-time SSD staff was hired. Student volunteers also offered support. Services were designed to give disabled students a learning environment with reasonable accommodations for disabilities.

Licensing the University of Texas logos and symbols gained new importance in the 1980s and 1990s. The licensing began in 1981, earned $31,000 in its first year, and reached over a half million dollars in 1990.

The University of Texas System, which coordinates the registration, has more trademark registrations than any other university system in the United States. Certain items such as alcoholic beverages, sexually suggestive products, staple foods, stationery, and firearms, are refused the trademarks.

Long registration lines in the September Texas sun or the January cold disappeared with the inauguration of TEX (Telephone Enrollment eXchange), the computerized telephone registration system, which began in 1990. Students paid an additional four dollar student service fee to cover the cost of new equipment. After a few glitches the first year, the system worked well, and a tremendous amount of time and effort were saved. Vice President for Graduate Studies and Research William S. Livingston, was the original voice for TEX and always closed his remarks to the students with, "Goodbye and good luck."

The College of Business began a massive campaign in the early 1990s to cut its enrollment in half. The long-time goal of the program was to provide a better education to business students and decrease the student-faculty ratio to twenty students per faculty member. Undergraduate enrollment in 1990 was 8,245 students.

Note: By 1995 it was 4,358. The reduction in size required tighter admissions standards.

After seventy-two years of producing oil, the Santa Rita # 1, UT's first oil and gas contributor to the Permanent University Fund (the discovery well), was finally plugged in May 1990.

Note: The old rig had been removed from the well in January 1940 and shipped to Austin. Finally, on a cool, rainy Thanksgiving Day, November 27, 1958, Texas and Texas A&M were preparing for a nationally televised football game. Just before kick-off, they took time out to memorialize Santa Rita. That rig still stands on the campus at the corner of Trinity and Martin Luther King, Jr., Boulevard.

The UT Ex-Students' Association raised $6.5 million in donations in order to expand the Lila B. Etter Alumni Center. Construction beside Waller Creek began in November 1988, and the new part of the building was opened on September 22, 1990. The newly renovated center, across the street from Memorial Stadium, contained a banquet hall capable of seating five hundred guests for dinner and a Texas Exes plaza with names of donors of bricks. The Association itself funded the complete renovation.

The Undergraduate Advising Center was set up on the first floor of the Flawn Academic Center in 1991. The Center has offered advising to undeclared undergraduates and to students enrolling at UT through provisional programs. Dr. Alice Reinarz was named director.

Note: In October 1995 the Center received an Outstanding Advising Award from the National Academic Advising Association. It has become a working model for the creation of campus-wide standards. Therefore, in 1995,

Executive Vice President and Provost Mark Yudof created the Provost's Council on Academic Advising to give impetus for overhauling the entire undergraduate advising program.

In September 1992 Dr. William H. Cunningham left the presidency after nine years (1984-1992) to succeed Dr. Hans Mark as chancellor of the University of Texas System. As he left, he listed these as highlights of his administration:

(1) decline of the student-faculty ratio, due to the addition of faculty resources and the positive effects of the enrollment management program;

(2) rise in the quality of undergraduates;

(3) improvement of facilities to enhance campus life: conversion of Carothers Dormitory into an undergraduate honors residence hall; the completion of the Recreational Sports Center; renovation of Wooldridge Hall for the Office of Student Financial Services; renovation of the Texas Union; and the planning of a new Student Services Building and a new Student Health Center;

(4) implementation of the recommendations of two special committees, one on the Undergraduate Student Experience and the other an Ad Hoc Committee on Undergraduate Education.

After President Cunningham left, the Regents named Dr. William S. Livingston, vice president and dean of graduate studies, as acting president, beginning September 5, 1992. He had been instrumental in the development of the LBJ School of Public Affairs, the Faculty Seminar in British Studies, the Clark Center for Australian Studies, the Normandy Scholars Program, and the Center for Writers. Livingston served as acting president until Dr. Robert Berdahl was elected and assumed the position in 1993.

The Joseph D. Jamail Center for Legal Research was dedicated on November 12, 1992. It includes the Tarlton Law Library, the Center for Computer Research and Instruction, the Texas Research Center for Child Abuse and Neglect, and two new law library fellowships. It was named for Joseph D. Jamail, who received a B. A. in 1950 and a law degree in 1952, both from UT. The Tarlton Law Library, fifth largest academic law library in the nation, is considered the finest legal research center in the Southwest.

The Texas Swimming Center was renamed the Lee and Joe Jamail Swimming Center in 1993.

In November 1992 Dr. Robert M. Berdahl from the University of Illinois was selected as president of the University. He was chosen by the Board of Regents from a field of finalists recommended by an advisory committee. He assumed the office at the beginning of 1993.

Since becoming president, among other things, he has stressed ways to improve a sense of community on campus, appointed a committee to draw a plan for campus development, and changed admission standards. Some of his programs to enhance a feeling of community have been "Longhorn Halloween," "Orange Santa," "Hearts of Texas Campaign," "Mooove In," "Home Team," and "Take Your Child To Work Day."

On March 30, 1994, the UT System Board of Regents named the Balcones Research Center for J. J. "Jake" Pickle, alumnus and former congressman from the district in which Austin and UT are located. In the 1980s UT began a $62 million expansion at Balcones, along with the construction of a $20 million building for the Microelectronics and Computer Technology Corporation (MCC). The fusion of research and development at the site has spawned numerous private companies currently operating in Austin and Central Texas.

Today the facility has a staff of about seven hundred, including nearly three hundred engineers and scientists, and its annual budget is in the range of $40 to $50 million. The bulk of the research program through the years has been sponsored by Department of Defense agencies, and the laboratory has made significant contributions to the better understanding of sonar, electromagnetics, and computer engineering.

Construction of the William P. Hobby–Robert E. Eberly Telescope, an innovative scientific tool, began on March 25, 1994, with a groundbreaking ceremony at McDonald Observatory in the Davis Mountains of West Texas. When completed, the telescope will be one of the world's largest and most powerful. It is expected to become fully operational by late 1997.

The University celebrated the centennial of Longhorn athletics, beginning in 1992. It consisted of a series of special events and activities spanning over a year. The first time a Texas college played a football game against outside opposition was The University of Texas versus a club from Dallas on Thanksgiving Day, 1893.

The University holds national football championships from 1963, 1969, and 1970, and has the most wins in conference play since Southwest Conference play began. Texas, Notre Dame, and Michigan are the three teams that have won the most games in college football history.

The entire athletic program is recognized nationally as being among the best. In 1984 the entire program was recognized as the best in the country by the National Collegiate All-Sports rankings, compiled by Steve Willis of the *Knoxville Journal*. Longhorn athletics also placed first in 1982 and second in 1983, to become one of only three universities in the country to rank at the top twice in the fourteen-year history of the poll.

On February 25, 1994, UT Austin was authorized by the Board of Regents to merge with the Big Eight Athletic Conference. The change became effective in June 1996. Other Southwest Conference schools joining in the merger were Baylor University, Texas A&M University, and Texas Tech University. The name of the conference has been changed to the Big Twelve. Among the advantages of the move listed included (1) UT would be in a conference with more schools that have a commitment to highly competitive athletic programs in a wide range of both men and women's sports; and (2) it would be in a more homogenous grouping of institutions. The change meant that the 1995-1996 season was the last for the Southwest Conference.

Announced in February 1996 by the University System Board of Regents was a long-range plan to expand and improve Memorial Stadium and other athletic facilities. On August 29, 1996, the Board of Regents changed the name of Texas Memorial Stadium to "Darrell K. Royal - – Texas Memorial Stadium," in honor of the legendary retired coach of the Longhorns. Royal won national football championships in 1963, 1969, and 1970.

The Robert and Nancy Dedman Scholars Program began in 1994, funded by a $10 million endowment from the Dedmans. The scholarships are highly competitive. Within a few years, plans are to award fifty of the scholarships to entering students. The original stipend was

$7,000 per year for five years. A student must maintain a 3.5 grade point average to keep the scholarship.

Note: Ohter major four-year scholarships are the Texas Excellence Awards for Scholarship and Leadership that are awarded by the Ex-Students' Association. They are made possible by the contributions of the many Texas Exes who support The Eyes of Texas Annual Giving Club.

In the spring of 1995 UT President Berdahl and Executive Vice President and Provost Mark Yudof announced the creation of the Academy of Distinguished Teachers, one of the first of its type in the nation. Its purpose is to recognize and enhance teaching, particularly at the undergraduate level. Members were chosen on the basis of their outstanding teaching, their personal commitment to students and the learning process, and their ability to inspire and motivate students in the classroom. Twelve members were chosen the first year. The Academy is limited to eighty professors in active service, or roughly six percent of the tenured faculty.

Tax dollars appropriated by the twenty-fourth Texas legislature represents 24.87% of UT Austin's total 1995-1996 budget of $845.5 million. Other sources of funds are federal, state, other governmental and private grants; self-supporting auxiliary enterprises, such as the Texas Union, intercollegiate athletics, and residence halls; the Available University Fund, which is income earned on the investments of the Permanent University Fund; private gifts and endowment income; fees and tuition paid by students; and miscellaneous other sources.

In early 1995 Dr. John J. McKetta, former dean of the College of Engineering and a vice chancellor during the Harry Ransom administration, offered to return all of the salary he earned during his forty-nine years on the faculty, about $1 million, to the Department of Chemical Engineering if his former students would raise a matching amount. By October 1995 the matching funds had reached $1.2 million, and four thousand students still had not been contacted. McKetta explained that he made the challenge at a time of changing financial circumstances when state universities are faced with declining state support for education.

In the spring of 1996 the Campus Master Planning Committee joined the architectural team of Cesar Pelli and Associates of New Haven, Connecticut, to finalize a comprehensive architectural plan for the next thirty years. Physics professor Dr. Austin Gleeson chaired the committee of nineteen members, which was appointed by President Berdahl in early 1995. They expressed hope that after $1.1 million and fourteen months, the plan will begin to reclaim and even maintain the architectural integrity the University boasted during the Paul Cret period.

Note: The comprehensive plan has been highly publicized. Officials say that it is to be carefully monitored by those responsible for campus planning and development. A member of the UT System Board of Regents who chairs the Facilities Planning and Construction Committee says the plan is the key to realizing President Berdahl's vision of a nurturing, friendly campus. "The plan will serve as a guide to help keep us all focused on that vision in the years ahead."

The University announced in June 1996 that beginning in the fall of 1997, the long-standing practice of automatic admissions would be changed. Instead, all applications will be examined individually, using broader criteria. In addition to SAT scores, grades, and class standing in high school, admission officers will consider family background, obstacles overcome, extracurricular activities, and creative talents. Administrative officials noted that the new system is another step to fulfill the legislative mandate, the creation of a "university of the first class." An important measure of a university's excellence is the quality of its students.

In March 1996 the US Circuit Court of Appeals ruled in the *Hopwood v. Texas* case that The University of Texas law school's affirmative action program is unconstitutional. (In 1992 an Austin lawyer filed a reverse discrimination lawsuit against the UT School of Law, charging that the UT law school's admission policies unfairly discriminated against white applicants. Cheryl Hopwood was the applicant whose name the case carries.) Texas Attorney General Dan Morales filed an appeal with the US Suprememm Court in April 1996 requesting *certiorari*. Then on July 1, 1996, the US Supreme Court announced that it would let stand the lower court ruling (denied *certiorari*); that, in effect, will eliminate affirmative action at the University. This decision promted another crisis in UT's development.

On March 6, 1997, President Robert Berdahl announced that he would leave The University of Texas at the end of June to assume the position as chancellor of the University of California at Berkeley. A popular president who was an excellent, innovative administrator, his leaving was generally regretted.

Note: Executive Vice President and Provost Mark Yudof, UT No. 2 officer, resigned in January 1997 to accept the presidency of the University of Minnesota. His legacy includes increasing academic advising of students, installing a performance-based instruction system for departments, increasing opportunities for students to study abroad, and honoring outstanding teachers through creation of the Academy of Distinguished Teachers. He was also instrumental in altering the tenure system for faculty and beginning programs to improve undergraduate education.

Following President Berdahl's resignation in March, Chancelor William H. Cunningham announced that Dr. Peter Tyrrell Flawn, UT president from 1979 until 1985, would return to the campus to serve as interim president. President Flawn's leadership and scholarship and accomplishments during his presidency made him a popular choice for the interim position. The Chancellor appointed a committee, which he will chair, composed of administrators, faculty, staff, alumni, and students, to begin an immediate search for a new president of UT Austin.

UT now: Science, Engineering, Allan Bean (UT ex) on the moon with school song, Santa Rita #1 well, Marine Studies in Galveston, McDonald Observatory with new HET.

Campus theatre club—Turn of the Century.
Helen Marr Kirby, Dean of Women, didn't like for girls to
participate in the campus theatre. When the Ashbel
Literary Society presented its annual show at the turn of
the century, she erected a waist-high wall across the front
of the stage to preserve maidenly dignity.

PART II

STUDENT CULTURE

STUDENT CULTURE

1880s

· Student life from a modern perspective was far from exciting. It was unorganized, slow paced, and often tiresome in its rural, pastoral setting.

· Students took buggy rides along trails that later became busy thoroughfares.

· Afternoons were often spent along the banks of Waller Creek, where low tree branches tangled the high coiffures of the girls, and the tall grass swished against their long full-gored skirts.

· Social and educational experiences included hikes to Mount Bonnell, pecan hunts, and class excursions to San Antonio, Marble Falls, and Barton's Creek.

· Time-honored traditions were established with class day and commencement exercises.

· Before the University was ten days old, two literary societies, the Athenaeum and the Rusk, were organized.

· Students had literary clubs before they had a baseball club.

· Fraternities were welcomed to the campus as soon as the University opened, because they provided housing for young men. Sororities, however, were prohibited.

· Groups of young men formed "mess clubs" to cut

expenses. The clubs were a distinctive feature of student life during the first decade of University operation.

· The University Drug Store, operated by P. W. McFadden and Claude E. Hill, was the first business establishment on the area of Guadalupe later known as the Drag.

· The beautiful Driskill Hotel opened at Christmas in 1886. It was the site of numerous student dances.

· Lamme's Candies opened on Congress Avenue in 1885 and sold generations of students "Gem," sugar stick candy, kisses, chewy pralines, and divinity.

. Students (only the men, of course) liked to spend afternoons sipping beer at tables under the big trees at Scholz's Beer Garten, with its adjacent Saengerrunde Halle. A resident big green parrot spoke freely of the morals of prominent students and faculty members, as well as the state's political leaders.

· Before a baseball game with Southwestern University in Georgetown in 1885, students passed out orange and white ribbons, thus using for the first time colors that later became official.

· The campus was covered with mesquite trees and a few live oaks. Here and there a cactus appeared. In the spring, bluebonnets and other wildflowers covered the Forty Acres.

· A plank fence was built around the Forty Acres to keep out cows and other stray animals.

· Money worries plagued students as much then as now.

· Issues included the need for increased space, smaller classes, curriculum changes, new grading systems, and library expansion.

· Freshmen and junior law students had their annual battles. "Cane rushes," common on East Coast campuses, were not tolerated at the University, but organized horseplay served similar ends.

· The class of 1892 began a practice, followed for a few years, of burning their hated Latin texts at the end of the school year.

· A Bryan Club and a Gold Club, representing the two major national political movements of the time, appeared on campus in 1896.

· One day in the spring of 1896, students met in a quiet and dignified way to adopt resolutions concerning the failure on the part of University Regents to re-elect a physics professor. This incident was the first student protest on campus.

· On March 2, 1897, a boisterous group of students, led by the senior law class, left their books to celebrate Texas Independence Day.

· The Final Ball, usually held at the Driskill Hotel, climaxed the extracurricular activities of the year. All classes spent time, effort, and money preparing for the special occasion, and male students vied for chairmanship of the ball.

· A football team was first organized in 1892. In 1893 the University enjoyed an undefeated season, its first, consisting of only four games.

· During the late 1890s, excursions to Dallas for the big football game during the Dallas Fair became popular.

· The *Cactus* yearbook was first published in 1894. This began the documentation of the University student culture that is marked significantly by changes closely related to the wider Texas culture.

· B. Hall, the first dormitory, opened in 1890. It was a major step in reducing costs and in promoting closer relationships among male students.

· In 1893 the Academic Department began exempting from all fees the valedictorians of "affiliated" high schools, those schools that met University entrance qualifications.

· The Episcopal Church opened the Young Ladies Church Institute in 1895 and offered a church home in Grace Hall in 1897 to a limited number of girls attending the University. (The University did not yet provide housing for women.)

· Students had fudge parties, tacky parties, and geographical charades parties.

· Going to see a fortune teller was a pastime, especially among co-eds.

· Attending productions at the Hancock Opera House or Saturday night "germans" at Saengerrunde Halle were occasional treats for students.

· At Grace Hall the women could go out on Saturday and Sunday nights but had to be in by 10:00 P.M. Hall lights were turned out at 11:00.

· In December 1895 students initiated publication of a newspaper, the *Alcalde*. Another newspaper, the *Calendar*, merged with the *Alcalde* in 1900 to become the *Texan*, a weekly at first.

· The outbreak of the Spanish-American War during the last weeks of the 1898 term, and epidemics of dengue and yellow fever, aroused mild excitement among students at the turn of the century.

1900s

· Renewed interest in student participation in University governance resulted in the organization of a students' council.

· The *Texan*, a weekly at first, became a bi-weekly beginning in 1907.

· The new student government assumed control of student publications, the annual March 2 celebration, and the annual all-students' outing on April 21 by train to Landa Park in New Braunfels, sixty miles from Austin.

· Mess clubs provided friendship groups for young men, as well as reduced living expenses.

· Charlie's Confectionery on the Drag was a favorite hangout for University students. More than a business, it was a study hall, a meeting place, and a social center.

· The first fraternity houses near the campus were built in 1902. Action of the fraternities was praised by University officials as "a move in the right direction."

· The first women's dormitory, the Woman's Building, opened in 1903.

· Sororities first appeared on campus in 1902, without the approval of Helen Marr Kirby, dean of women. Four years later, she joined one.

· President and Mrs. William L. Prather had "at homes," honoring class groups.

· Saturday night "germans," dances sponsored originally by the German Club, were popular.

· Residents of the Woman's Building held Sunday night receptions, to which the residents wore long dresses and stood in a receiving line.

· Residents of B: Hall enjoyed long after-dinner oratory, practical jokes, and midnight initiations for membership in secret organizations.

· Fraternities and sororities provided most of the campus social life. Dances, banquets, "at homes," teas, excursions, picnics, and "candy-pulls" were popular.

· A trolley party was always fun and inexpensive. Students would ride the trolley its entire round, and perhaps end with a party at somebody's home, or simply stop at Sixth and Congress for popcorn and other refreshments.

· The Final Ball continued to be the grand climax of campus social events.

· Commencement Week social activities became so numerous and expensive that the faculty passed a resolution to limit them.

· On May 26, 1906, a Charity Circus served as a benefit for the Athletic Council. The second benefit, called Varsity Circus, featured the election of a queen and a parade.

Note: The Varsity Circus occurred biennially until the one in 1925, when the Students' Association abolished it.

· The Longhorn Band was organized in the fall of 1900 by Dr. Eugene P. Schoch. It appeared for the first time at the Kansas City–Texas football game. The first uniforms were white smocks.

· The Curtain Club, the oldest drama organization at the University, was founded in 1909 by Stark Young. The club was strictly extracurricular.

· Beginning in 1904 or 1905, nightshirt parades were popular before and after football games and other important campus events.

1910s

· Automobiles first appeared on campus about 1907 or 1908, when football teams were escorted on field by students in automobiles. Lutcher Stark, in 1911, was the first student to own an automobile. That they were becoming a factor in student life was indicated by traffic regulations on campus announced as early as January 1914.

· Library dates were popular during the school week. When lights blinked at 8:45, students closed their books and, with their dates, walked the Perip (the walk around the Forty Acres) or would go to Schutze's Cozy Corner at 24th and Guadalupe or Charlie's Confectionery at 23rd for a thick chocolate malted milk, oyster loaf, or chili and hot tamales.

· "Germans," held downtown at the Knights of Columbus hall, were big social events. Girls wore long evening dresses and carried their slippers in an evening bag. Program dances were popular.

· The Car Shed, where students waited to board a street-car on the west side of the campus, was a landmark. Students often met there for picnics or to make preparation for parades.

· Beck's Pond was a shallow puddle about three feet wide along the graveled walk on the northwest side of what is now Battle Hall. Crude as it was, it was a lovers' rendezvous on the campus.

· Students marched to the Governor's Mansion in April 1914 and urged the governor to send them to guard the Mexican border when Pancho Villa was making raids into Texas.

. Students protested Gov. James E. Ferguson's actions toward the University in May 1917, and marched to the Capitol to voice the protest.

· Stephen Pinckney, a 1911 graduate, collected one dollar each from one hundred twenty-four alumni and purchased a Longhorn steer to be the University mascot. It arrived in Austin in late November 1916, and at the Thanksgiving game was presented to students of The University of Texas. He was named Bevo.

· Numerous students left the University to participate in World War I in 1917. The Loyalty Day parade was "the biggest parade ever held in Austin" until that time.

· East Woods on Waller Creek was a popular picnic spot, and West Woods (present day Tarrytown) was often the destination of hikers. An extended jaunt might end at the dam or Mount Bonnell. A date to walk on a pretty afternoon was more popular than a streetcar ride downtown to a picture show.

· Ribbon Clubs (interfraternity organizations) sponsored the most elaborate dances. The Greeks also sponsored numerous informal affairs, such as canoe trips, picnics, hikes, stunt parties, "baby" parties, smokers, and stag banquets.

· The YMCA and YWCA had picnics twice a year, in the fall and in the spring, in East Woods. There they built a huge bonfire and roasted bacon and marshmallows over the coals and sang popular songs.

· The Freshman Reception, the Sophomore Reception, Junior Week, the Academic Reception, the Law Banquet, the Engineer's Open House and Banquet, and senior activities during Commencement Week were annual class and departmental social affairs.

1920s

· The moral revolt of the "jazz age" was a factor affecting student life in the 1920s. Writers attributed the change to "the war, the motorcar, Freud and bootleg gin."

· Mores of women changed. Female students bobbed their hair, shortened their skirts, smoked in public, and danced all the new steps to music of the jazz bands.

· Social life at the University received more attention in the press than did academic accomplishments. Some one hundred-fifty clubs, societies, and groups were on campus, while enrollment was only five thousand. Fraternities and sororities were strong forces on campus and heavily influenced student culture.

· Fraternities devised all kinds of activities for initiations. Hazing was rampant.

· Interest in athletics soared. The yell leader and his assistants held positions of prominence. Huge pre-game rallies aroused student interest.

· Society pages of the *Daily Texan* described dinner parties, luncheons, buffet suppers, smokers, banquets, and 'possum hunts. Dancing was the most popular activity. An all-University dance, called the "german," was usually held in the Women's Gymnasium on Saturday nights.

· Old "flivvers," used cars students bought for $35 to $100, were a fad during the middle and late 1920s.

· On dates, students went to a dance or movie, went automobile riding, or sat in a porch swing or a dormitory lounge and talked or listened to a Victrola or a radio, or played cards.

· In the spring students had picnics, swimming parties, went canoeing, or to Bull Creek to broil a steak, or for twenty-five cents per car parked at Dillingham's pasture, located off the turnpike toward Georgetown, where Mr. Dillingham served as security guard and curfew caller.

· Guadalupe Streets between 21st and 24th streets, called "The Drag," had drug stores, hamburger stands, cafes, and fruit shops. Drug stores were gathering places for students with an hour or so between classes. Students might drive up to the curb, honk the horn, and receive curb service for their cherry Cokes, limeades, chocolate sodas, or "java."

· New terms were in popular use: flappers, jelly beans, bell-bottom trousers, Oxford bags, Valentino pants, one-piece bathing suits, bobbed hair, short skirts, making whoopee, jazz, the Charleston, flash card stunts, crossword puzzles, comics, chewing gum, aeroplane rides, slang, Sunday movies, co-ed smoking, barnyard golf.

· Junior women dressed as men and escorted formally attired senior women to a Junior Prom.

· Dirty Martin's opened in 1926 *[and is still thriving seventy years later]*. A "Kum-bak" hamburger was a special treat.

· Student government concerned itself with chartering Texas Student Publications, Inc., raising money for Memorial Stadium, celebrating the University's fortieth anniversary, designing and adopting the first official senior ring, abolishing the honor system, and planning the Student Union drive (including Gregory Gymnasium, Women's Gymnasium, and Hogg Auditorium).

1930s

· Signs of the nationwide Depression appeared on campus in the early 1930s.

· Flashy roadsters were replaced with cooperatively owned "flivvers," low-priced rooms were in demand, and bookstores found an increasing market for secondhand books.

· Hitchhiking was a national pastime.

· Girls chose cotton dresses for formals and asked dates not to buy corsages.

· The twenty-five-cent lunch was popular.

· Both ice cream and chewing gun were sold in abundance at places along the Drag.

· Jigsaw puzzles and comic strips were popular.

· More "democratic" dances every Saturday night in Gregory Gymnasium (and later in the Texas Union) replaced those formerly sponsored by the Ribbon clubs and various town groups.

· The annual Round-Up Ball was a special event. Round-Up, a spring festival to bring alumni back to the campus, was first held in 1930. Round-Up parades began in 1934, and each year the parade became bigger.

· During the Depression years, March 2 and April 1 celebrations became less rowdy; student interests were changing.

· Movies increased in popularity.

· "Road houses" appeared on the outskirts of town, and students were good customers.

· "Navajo (blanket) parties," especially at Dillingham's pasture, were listed as "probably the most famous and most popular of Texas traditions."

· Radios blared swing music of Paul Whiteman and Glenn Miller from open windows in non-air-conditioned dormitories and boarding houses.

· Students attended tea dances in the Texas Union and danced to the music of Benny Goodman and Guy Lombardo.

· "Stags" (men without dates) at dances provided students the opportunity to meet new friends. Being "stuck" with one dancer was an embarrassment to both students.

· Hilsberg's at 101 East 21st Street was a good place to get a steak, and Wukasch's at 2002 Guadalupe was a favorite place for Sunday dinner (for fifty cents).

· Miss Anna Jansen presided at the University Commons, where her fried chicken was twenty-five cents and a big slice of devil's food cake was ten cents.

· Women paid an average of $12.41 for room and $26.09 for board per month; men averaged $10.39 for room and $23.84 for board.

· Most of the powers of student government once given to the students had been gradually withdrawn by University administrators as the student body grew larger, so that student interest in student government lagged.

· The principal responsibilities of the Students' Assembly during the 1930s were to elect a representative to the Athletic Council, elect two members of the Publication Board, appropriate all monies of the Students' Association, apportion the Blanket Tax proceeds among certain organizations, and plan arrangements for student celebrations.

1940s

· Female enrollment was greater than that of males after

World War II began. A woman was elected *Daily Texan* editor in 1944, and another became president of the student body in 1945 when the male incumbent resigned to enter the military service.

· Dim-out regulations darkened the Tower for two years, and the Tower chimes were silent for a while when the University had no carillonneur.

· Gasoline and sugar rationing changed the lifestyles of both students and faculty.

· Victory gardens were popular.

· The Students' Association conducted bond selling campaigns.

· Numerous marriages occurred before the young men left for the service.

· Women were admitted to the Longhorn Band, but they did not yet wear uniforms or march in the band at athletic events.

· A Navy V-12 training unit was established in 1943; a V-5 program was in existence for a while. In 1945 a Reserve Officers Training Corps (ROTC) was established with the same status as other departments in the University. All three units of the armed forces at the time were represented on campus, and military uniforms were common.

· Counseling and advisory facilities were improved. In 1946 the Students' Association made an investigation of the Student Health Service, comparing it with other university health services, and ultimately submitting a report to University officials. The study resulted in expanded health services, including a new building in 1950.

· Special places for students to eat included the University Tea House, opened on campus in 1939, and listed by Duncan Hines in his *Adventures in Good Eating*; Green Pastures, which was to become one of Austin's finest restaurants; and El Matamoros at 504 East Avenue.

· A lighting system was installed on the intramural sports playing fields in 1947 (where Jester Center is now located). The Interfraternity Council contributed $11,000 to the project, and the Athletic Council paid the balance, approximately $29,000.

· In these pre-television days, the Texas Union and Alpha Phi Omega sponsored Grid-Graph parties, play-by-play reports of out-of-town football games. Large groups of students gathered at the Union or in Gregory Gymnasium or in front of the University Co-Op to "watch" a game.

· Round-Up parades became spectacular events. The 1947 parade featured fifty-four floats.

· Student government was active and important in the late 1940s. Student elections were marked by the revival of the old-time pre-war spirit and noisy activity.

· As the decade ended, young men were once again involved in war, this time in Korea.

1950s

· Students rocked to Elvis Presley, enjoyed James Dean and Marlon Brando, and read Dylan Thomas poetry.

· Bigness was cheered: big enrollment, big band, big dances, big Round-Up parade and review, big Varsity Carnival, big fraternities and sororities, big ROTC, big black-faced Cowboy minstrels. Extracurricular activities blossomed.

· Old B. Hall was finally razed in 1952, much to the dismay of some sentimental alumni.

· Students conducted "Steer Here" campaigns to try to desegregate businesses on the Drag.

· "Smokey," the spirit cannon, was built in 1953 by some students in Mechanical Engineering.

· The "Hook 'em Horns" signal was introduced by head cheerleader Harley Clark in Gregory Gymnasium at a pep rally before the TCU football game in 1955. His good friend, Henry Pitts, suggested the sign.

· "Big Bertha," reportedly the world's largest drum, became a part of the Longhorn Band in 1955. It originally belonged to the University of Chicago, which no longer played football and didn't need the drum.

· Girls in penny loafers and white socks and with full skirts supported by crinoline petticoats and boys with ducktail and flat-top haircuts were described as "conformists" by critics of the campus culture.

· Jitterbugging was the popular style of dancing.

· Sock hops, western hops, and big formals filled the campus social calendar, which was kept in the office of the dean of student life.

· Chaperones began to go out of style.

· Students gathered in groups to watch television, including the McCarthy hearings in 1954.

· Torchlight parades down the Drag before each pep rally in the fall were led by the Longhorn Band, Bevo, the Silver Spurs, and the Cowboys, and were followed by large numbers of students.

· In May 1952 the University community experienced its first panty raid, a fad on college campuses that had a big build-up in national magazines and full coverage in newspapers across the country.

· Varsity football stirred more enthusiasm than any other activity. Following a football game, the entire campus community became a beehive of activity that included dances, beer-busts, backyard parties, and church socials.

· A freshman car ban caused loud student protests.

· Student expenses, not counting incidentals, averaged between $442 and $725 in 1950-1951.

· Before the 1950s ended, the Russians sent Sputnik into space, and its impact brought significant cultural changes to the campus.

1960s

· Young people of university age were more numerous, more influential, healthier, and even wealthier than their predecessors.

· Students began to focus on aspects of institutional hypocrisy, social discrimination, and an unpopular war.

· Like Texas society, the University student culture was in painful transition.

. The early 1960s were not unlike the 1950s; student life was fast-paced and over-organized; fraternity and sorority members comprised less than one-third of the student body, but they provided the leadership of planned frivolity; Round-Up was a week-long rite that mirrored the University's many faces; the big trek to Dallas for the Texas–Oklahoma football game was a rite in itself; placards placed on trees recommended that students learn "the Twist, the Jitterbug, and the Dallas Push."

· Sing-Song, water-skiing, Varsity Carnival, weekly dances, formals, beer parties, and endless queen contests characterized the period.

· Girls seldom thought of graduate study. The teased hair-dos (fluffheads) and short miniskirts were uniforms of the period.

· The pageantry of Memorial Stadium during a football game included artifacts of the student culture: Bevo, the mascot; Smokey, the cannon; Bertha, the drum; and the gigantic Texas flag, a gift from the governor of Mississippi after the Cotton Bowl game in 1962.

· The Vietnam War and the assassinations of John F. Kennedy, Martin Luther King, Jr., and Robert Kennedy had a sobering influence on student thought and behavior.

· *In loco parentis* became a dead concept, if only because University growth outstripped the growth of University housing.

· Many students chose to live in apartments in old houses with wooden floors and fenced backyards for their dogs.

85

· To avert protests occurring on other campuses across the country, UT students were given a greater voice in policy-making; students were added to the University Council.

· Most students were conservative and a majority were lethargic, but the Students for a Democratic Society (SDS) was a small but noisy group that produced leaders in the national movement against the Vietnam War.

· Only about two hundred African-Americans were enrolled in any one semester during the 1960s, but housing and University athletics were desegregated.

· The impact of the Charles Whitman incident on August 2, 1966, on the student body was sobering.

· "Street people," often having no connection with the University, appeared in large numbers and used the Texas Union as a hangout. These "hippies" and "flower children" sold wares along the Drag.

· Stump speaking, Gentle Thursdays, and Flipped-Out Weeks were frequent.

· Sororities and a few fraternities no longer registered as official University organizations because they refused to say they did not discriminate.

· The environment was an issue. Students celebrated Earth Day and became "natural food freaks," searched out health food stores, and did organic gardening in community gardens or on their patios.

· Youth power, student activism, the black power movement, the women's movement, the "God is Dead" movement, the hippie-yippie movement, and the pot culture all produced major changes in students' values, goals, and priorities.

· Drugs were a pervasive problem.

· On November 10, 1969, students, non-students, Department of Public Safety officers, and Austin police had a confrontation inside and around the Chuck Wagon at the Texas Union. Eight persons, including five students, were arrested. Later, at least twenty-two others were arrested and named in grand jury indictments.

1970s

· Social changes in the 1960s had a significant effect on the campus of the 1970s.

· Noticeable surges of change included the anti-war movement, widespread use of drugs, including alcohol, integration efforts, use of the pill, campus revolts, and various anti-elitist movements.

· Demonstrations and protests became routine and commonplace at the University in the early 1970s.

· Students at the University protested the Vietnam War, the Kent State killings, the firing of Dean John Silber, the building of Bauer House for the chancellor, the construction of a wall around part of the campus, digging up the West Mall in preparation for new landscaping, the firing of President Stephen Spurr, the hiring of Lorene Rogers as president, cutting the trees on Waller Creek to make room for the expansion of Memorial Stadium, Texas abortion laws, keeping non-students out of the Texas Union, and the possibility of males being drafted.

· Students demonstrated for the rights of blacks, Chicanos,

women, the mobility impaired, married students, veterans, and foreign students.

· The voting age was lowered in 1971 from 21 to 18. Most students were then adults; the University no longer stood *in loco parentis.*

· More older students, especially women, returned to classes.

· Assertiveness training and consciousness-raising sessions were popular in the early 1970s.

· Title IX of the 1972 Education Amendments led service and honor organizations to become co-ed and helped women's athletics begin to get financial support.

· Alcohol was permitted on campus in 1974; even the Texas Union began to sell beer, wine, and mixed drinks.

· Co-ed floors were organized in Jester Center, a dormitory complex that housed over three thousand students.

· The Watergate scandals, the resignation of President Richard Nixon, the serious energy shortage, and spiraling inflation all cast a gloomy shadow on the campus.

· Early in the 1970s psychology was the most popular major.

· For the first time, a woman was elected president of the Students' Association. She was Carol Crabtree.

· After the Vietnam War ended, changing economic conditions caused students to be more career-oriented, and business administration was the most attractive field of study.

· Enrollment climbed from thirty-nine thousand in 1970 to more than forty-four thousand in 1979.

· The shuttle bus, started in the 1960s, was extremely popular, and many students rode bicycles and mopeds.

· With increasing costs of rent and food, students moved back to the residence halls, which had been unpopular in the late 1960s.

· The Students' Association, after seventy-six years, was dumped by popular vote of the student body in 1978. Proclaiming it a farce, serious student leaders urged its defeat.

· New centers of interest for students emerged in the Alumni Center, where a Student Involvement Committee became visible and active.

· The newly renovated Texas Union attracted student interest again, but the Union was plagued with financial problems, and students in general grew tired of requests for fee increases.

· Fraternities and sororities enjoyed a comeback during the second half of the decade, but they had to combat continuing criticism for their non-integrated memberships, their conservative lifestyles, their hazing, and their parties.

· Drag vendors occupied so much space on Guadalupe in the early 1970s that they were moved to 23rd Street (the Renaissance Market), where the city closed the street to traffic and widened the sidewalks.

· The Varsity and Texas theaters shifted from first-run films to increasingly risque and X-rated pictures. By the end of the decade, both closed as theaters.

· Food vendors on the Drag and at other popular campus crosswalks sold sandwiches, egg rolls, fajitas, burritos, cookies, and homemade ice cream. The Schlotzsky, a wonderful giant-size sandwich first made in the 1960s at a shop on South Congress, was a student favorite.

· Discos drew big crowds. Students filled Valentine's, the Greenhouse, and the Keg any night of the week. Country western music flourished. The Broken Spoke and Silver Dollar North and South were extremely popular on "student nights."

· Rock, hard rock, and rock-a-billy blared from stereos and loud speakers in the student neighborhoods.

· The crowd that heard the rock band, ZZ Top, in Memorial Stadium in September 1973 almost ruined the artificial turf.

· The once-popular Night Hawk on the Drag, Christi's on Town Lake, and El Mat on East Avenue, victims of changing times, closed in the late 1970s.

· Jeans, t-shirts, and sandals dominated the fashion picture of the 1970s for both males and females. Skimpy bikinis and even topless swimsuits were seen at Barton Springs, around apartment complex pools, and at Hippie Hollow on Lake Travis.

· Toward the end of the 1970s, students appeared neater as girls began to wear skirts and blouses, Mexican dresses, and sun dresses to class and men wore button-down collars and Izod shirts with jeans and slacks instead of cutoffs.

· The Tower turned orange to salute football championships, Nobel Prize winner Ilya Prigogine, Heisman Trophy recipient Earl Campbell, and the UT Press's bestseller, *The Book of Merlyn*.

· Concerns on campus about the environment and energy, about drugs, values, and the nuclear family, and about making money all spilled over from the so-called "outside world."

1980s

· The size and composition of the student body (more than forty-six thousand in 1981 and from every state in the US and ninety countries), the size of the campus (three hundred-sixteen contiguous acres with approximately one hundred-thirty buildings), the quality of teaching, the superb libraries, and laboratories all combined to provide an enriched environment.

· The social revolution of the 1960s and 1970s leveled off in the 1980s, as campus life became more reserved.

· More students described themselves as conservative.

· They were less likely to favor the legalization of marijuana.

· Students were more career-motivated than ever before. Holding a job while getting a degree was a common practice.

· The proposed average budget for a single undergraduate Texas resident in 1981-1982 was $5,000 and for a non-resident, single undergraduate was $6,000.

· Expensive, privately owned condominiums were "in," especially for upper-division students.

· These 1980s students, like those in the rest of the country, were often labeled as the "me generation."

· Students began registering in the air-conditioned Frank C. Erwin Special Events Center, but by the end of the decade they registered by telephone and computer, with the assistance of "TEX."

· Students worked hard and played hard. They danced at the Silver Dollar and drank at Scholz's, Bean's, Raul's, the County Line, and Dry Creek.

· They enjoyed the bars, night clubs, and restaurants on Sixth Street, and participated enthusiastically in the University's excellent intramural sports program.

· Football was still the favorite intercollegiate sport, but basketball, baseball, volleyball, and swimming drew crowds when teams were highly competitive.

· Women's athletics, especially basketball and swimming, became popular as teams won championships.

· Big all-University parties at Fiesta Gardens on Town Lake, several miles from the campus, attracted as many as five thousand or six thousand students.

· Favorite bands included "Little Bit of Texas," "Uncle Walt's," and "Beto y los Fairlanes."

· A reversal of male-female roles began to occur as co-eds often asked men for dates.

· Big groups of students often got together in somebody's condo or apartment to have a meal, watch Home Box Office (HBO) films on television, or enjoy an evening of conversation (the bull sessions of yesteryear students).

· Barbeque and Mexican foods were still favorites.

· Favorite places for barbeque were the County Line, Coupland, or the Salt Lick.

· Unisex dress went to class, to parties, and even to work.

· Pot smoking was common. Drinking was also a norm, as it had been through the decades. The Texas legislature enacted a measure raising the minimum drinking age from eighteen to twenty-one. Whether or not one smoked or drank, however, was a personal choice, not a peer requirement.

· The more intimate personal relationship between the sexes publicized in the 1960s and continued in the 1970s still existed in the 1980s.

· Students traveled while they studied. A Mexican holiday in Puerta Vallarta, Acapulco, or Cancun, or a ski holiday on the slopes in Colorado or New Mexico was popular. A theater and museum trip to New York at Christmas, a summer tour of Europe, or a weekend on the beach at South Padre was not unusual.

· "Shooting the rapids" on the Guadalupe River at New Braunfels, as at the turn of the century but more commercialized, was popular.

· Not unusual was a trip to Laredo to visit the Cadillac Bar and to shop in the markets for Mexican-made crafts.

· Jogging on Town Lake, along Shoal Creek, or in Memorial Stadium was common. A fun-run sponsored by the Ex-Students' Association in the fall and the Capitol 10,000 in the spring attracted large numbers of students.

· KTSB, the UT cable-only radio station, opened in 1988.

It made progress on its way to FM airwaves and gained public awareness, if not approval.

· The Lady Longhorns of the women's basketball team were the sweethearts of everyone.

1990s

· Students showed more real interest in politics in the 1990s than in past decades.

· On any weeknight, students inhabited cozy coffeehouses and bakery shops near the campus. Quackenbush's on the Drag, opened in 1983, was popular, as were Texas French Bread, and Mojo's Daily Grind.

· The West Mall was still a potpourri of the unusual: protests from equal rights activists, speeches by environmentalists, political campaigns, serenades by unknown bands. Or it might be a place to relax with a cup of coffee or a soda, a place to meet an old friend or make a new one, or perhaps a place to sit and blow bubbles and think of nothing at all.

· Students on their way to class often stopped by Cafe Expresso at the Texas Union to buy coffee, cappuccino, Italian sodas, or pastries.

· Kiosks replaced the campus trees as places to display posters of all kinds. The project began in 1990 and by September 1992, twenty-five kiosks were erected.

· Multiculturalism, the environment, increasing tuition and fees, fraternity hazing, minority enrollment, the presidential elections, and vagrants on the Drag were some of the concerns of the student body.

· The role of the UT sweetheart was expanded. Actually, the name was changed to "Ambassador," and two were chosen, one female and one male. Communication skill, scholarship and activities, as well as a knowledge of UT traditions were among the criteria used to narrow the field of nominees.

· Students all over the country, including those at UT, became known as "Generation X," a generation without a cause, lost in the debris of past years.

· The University approved a system-wide smoke-free policy in June 1991, which went into effect on September 1, sparking a heated debate.

· Volunteerism was a way of life. A special volunteer office was opened. Students, in groups or individually, usually found some time to do community volunteer work.

· UT mechanical engineering students built and raced *Texas Native Sun*, completely powered by solar energy, from Epcot Center in Florida to Warren, Michigan (sixteen hundred miles) in eleven days.

· Students joined in cheering the Dallas Cowboys as they began holding their summer training camp across town at St. Edward's University in 1990.

· Most students had their own e-mail addresses and used regularly the hundreds of computers in various locations on campus.

· Barton Creek was a rendezvous for students seeking relaxation.

· Students joined Austin by recycling newspapers, glass, and empty cans.

· Racial tensions rose occasionally on the diverse campus, but student groups and forums materialized to give vent to feelings.

· Students joined other citizens at the beginning of the decade in having mixed emotions concerning UT involvement in the Middle East. Protest cries described the dilemma: "No blood for oil!" at one time, and "Support our troops; take out Saddam Hussein" at another.

· Rollerblading was extremely popular. Skating clubs appeared. Students skated on avenues, in parking garages and in downtown Austin, but not legally through the University campus. Rollerblades rented for $10 per day.

· Students spoke out against date rape and fraternity violence.

· Hazing was a big issue following several serious incidents. The Texas Cowboys, a University service organization and spirit group since 1922, was suspended from the campus until the year 2000.
    Note: And the Silver Spurs took over firing "Little Smokey" after the Longhorns scored at football games.

· Homeless teenagers along the Drag were a continuing problem. Estimates placed the number at three to four hundred.

· Cycling gained importance. Mountain biking, road-racing, cross country, or merely riding for exercise or relaxation was a special pastime.

· The Oasis on Lake Travis was a popular place to go for a brew and to watch the sun set.

· Tower Records bought the old Varsity Theater on the Drag.

· Murals appeared on near-campus or downtown buildings, painted on once blank walls.

· Body piercing and tatooing were fads.

· An official University ring was adopted.

· The Texas Union's food court was renovated.

· Cigar smoking became a "cool" pastime.

· The H.O.R.D.E. music festival each summer had a huge student turnout.

· Cedar Street, a jazz venue on 4th Street, was extremely popular.

· Student life at the University was not a self-contained experience; it was an *Austin* experience.

Students protest on Main Mall over Kent State shootings and invasion of Cambodia (1970).

APPENDIX

PRESIDENTS OF THE UNIVERSITY OF TEXAS AT AUSTIN

From the time the University opened in 1883 until 1895, The University of Texas did not have a president. A chairman of the faculty was the chief administrator. Dr. J. W. Mallet was chairman for the first year, 1883-1884. Then Dr. Leslie Waggener was chairman from 1884 until 1894. Dr. Thomas S. Miller served the next year, 1894-1895. Then, in 1895, the office of president was created. The following have served as presidents:

1895-1896	Leslie Waggener, M.A., LL.D., *ad interim*
1896-1899	George Taylor Winston, M.A., LL.D.
1899-1905	William Lambdin Prather, B.L., LL.D.
1905-1908	David Franklin Houston, M.A., LL.D.
1908-1914	Sidney Edward Mezes, Ph.D., LL.D.
1914-1916	William James Battle, Ph.D., D.C.L., LL.D., *ad interim*
1916-1923	Robert Ernest Vinson, D.D., LL.D.

1923-1924	William Seneca Sutton, M.A., LL.D., *ad interim*
1924-1927	Walter Marshall William Splawn, Ph.D., LL.D.
1927-1937	Harry Yandell Benedict, Ph.D., LL.D.
1937-1939	John William Calhoun, M.A., LL.D., *ad interim*
1939-1944	Homer Price Rainey, Ph.D., LL.D.
1944-1946	Theophilus Shickel Painter, Ph.D., D.Sc., LL.D., M.N.A.S., *Acting President*
1946-1952	Theophilus Schickel Painter, Ph.D., D.Sc., LL.D., M.N.A.S.
1952	James Clay Dolley, Ph.D., *Acting President*
1953-1960	Logan Wilson, Ph.D., LL.D.
1960-1961	Harry Huntt Ransom, Ph.D., Litt.D., LL.D., L.H.D.
1961	Harry Huntt Ransom, Ph.D., Litt.D., LL.D., L.H.D., *Acting President*
1961-1963	Joseph Royall Smiley, Ph.D.
1963-1967	*There was no president; the chancellor presided.*
1967-1970	Norman Hackerman, Ph.D.
1970-1971	Bryce Jordan, Ph.D., *ad interim*
1971-1974	Stephen H. Spurr, M.F., Ph.D., D.Sc.
1974-1975	Lorene Lane Rogers, PhD., D.Sc., F.A.I.C., *ad interim*
1975-1979	Lorene Lane Rogers, Ph.D., D.Sc., F.A.I.C.
1979-1985	Peter Tyrrell Flawn, Ph.D.
1985-1992	William H. Cunningham, Ph.D.
1992-1993	William S. Livingston, Ph.D., *Acting President*
1993-1997	Robert M. Berdahl, Ph.D.
1997-	Peter Tyrrell Flawn, Ph.D., *Acting President*

CHANCELLORS OF THE UNIVERSITY OF TEXAS SYSTEM

The Board of Regents exercises its powers and authorities in the governance of The University of Texas System through the Office of the Chancellor. The chancellorship was not created until 1950. Heads of the various component institutions (currently fifteen) hold the title of president. The University of Texas at Austin is the original — the flagship — component institution.

1950-1953	James Pinckney Hart, LL.D.
1954	Logan Wilson, Ph.D., LL.D., *Acting Chancellor*

Note: The chancellorship was abolished on September 30, 1954, and was not re-established until September, 1960.

1960-1961	Logan Wilson, Ph.D., LL.D.
1961-1970	Harry Huntt Ransom, Ph.D., Litt.D., LL.D., L.H.D.
1971-1978	Charles A. LeMaistre, M.D.
1978-1984	Everitt Donald Walker, C.P.A., LL.D.
1984-1992	Hans Mark, Ph.D.
1992-	William H. Cunningham, Ph.D.

PRESIDENTS OF THE STUDENTS' ASSOCIATION

1902	W. T. Bartholomew
1903-1904	Charles W. Ramsdell
1904-1905	Edward Crane
1905-1906	Frank M. Ryburn
1906-1907	L. W. Parrish
1907-1908	J. D. D. Cobb
1908-1909	H. B. "Tick" Seay

1909-1910	Towne Young
1910-1911	L. S. Hoffman
1911-1912	Richard Ernest Seagler
1912-1913	Hugh Potter
1913-1914	A. Garland Adair
1914-1915	E. H. Lawhon
1915-1916	Francis J. Lyons
1916-1917	Raymond Myers
1917-1918	Virgil P. Lee
1918-1919	Reagan R. Huffman
1919-1920	Wallace Hawkins
1920-1921	J. Benton Morgan
1921-1922	C. Read Granberry
1922-1923	Archie D. Gray
1923-1924	F. F. "Rube" Leissner
1924-1925	S. Eldon Dyer
1925-1926	Richard W. Blalock
1926-1927	Ed Gossett
1927-1928	Robert Eikel
1928-1929	Byron Skelton
1929-1930	Robert M. "Bob" Payne
1830-1931	Hugh D. Dunlap
1931-1932	Wilson H. Elkins
1932-1933	Allan Shivers
1933-1934	Hill Hodges
1934-1935	John J. Bell
1935-1936	Jenkins Garrett
1936-1937	Jimmy Brinkley
1937-1938	J. J. "Jake" Pickle
1937-1939	John B. Connally
1939-1940	Sydney Reagan
1940-1941	J. Ward Fouts
1941-1942	Fred Niemann
1942-1943	William Arthur "Bill" Barton
1943-1944	T. Lawrence "Larry" Jones
	Bill Booth
1944-1945	Malcolm E. "Mac" Wallace
	Anna Buchanan
1945-1946	Clayton E. Blakeway
	Richard Mollison

1946-1947	James W. "Jim" Smith
	Howard D. McElroy
	Fritz Lyne
1947-1948	Bradley Bouland
	John Fry
1948-1949	Harold Barefoot Sanders
1949-1950	Ellis Brown
1950-1951	Lloyd Hand
1951-1952	Wales H. Madden, Jr.
	Wilson Forman
1952-1953	Rush Moody
1953-1954	Franklin Spears
1954-1955	Jerry Wilson
1955-1956	Ray Farrabee
	Bob Siegal
	Roland Dahlin
1956-1957	Lloyd Leroy Hayes
1957-1958	Lloyd Leroy Hayes
1957-1958	Harley Clark
1958-1959	William Howard Wolf
1959-1960	Frank Claude Cooksey
1960-1961	R. Cameron Hightower
	Maurice S. Olian
1961-1962	Maurice S. Olian
1962-1963	Lowell Lebermann
	M. "Sandy" Sanford
1963-1964	Julius Glickman
1964-1965	Gregory O. Lipscomb
1965-1966	John Mack Orr
1966-1967	Clif Drummond
1967-1968	Lloyd Doggett
1968-1969	Rostam M. Kavoussi
1969-1970	Joseph R. Krier
1970-1971	Jeffery J. Jones
1971-1972	Robert Thomas Binder
1972-1973	Dick Benson
1973-1974	B. A."Sandy" Kress
1974-1975	Frank Fleming
1975-1976	Carol Ann Crabtree
1976-1977	James B. "Jay" Adkins

1977-1978   Judy Spalding
No president between 1978 and 1982.
1982-1983   Paul Edward Begala
1983-1984   M. R. "Mitch" Krindler
1984-1985   Rodney Schlosser
1985-1986   Scott Scarborough
1986-1987   Andrew Chen
               Blair Scholossberg
1987-1988   Randi Shade
1988-1989   Mike Hulbert
1989-1990   Jerry Haddican
1990-1991   Toni Luckett
1991-1992   Garth Davis
1992-1993   Howard Nirken
1993-1994   Eric Bradley
1994-1995   John S. Black
1995-1996   Sherry Boyles
1996-1997   Jeff Tsai

UT BUILDINGS

WITH DATES OF COMPLETION

Buildings that have been razed

Old Main Building (1883, 1889, 1899)
First Power Plant (1889)
B. Hall (1890)
Old Chemical Laboratory (1891)
Clark Field I (1896)
Woman's Building (1903)
Old Law Building (1908)
Second Power Plant (1910)
Twenty-four Shacks (1911-1935)
Little Campus Buildings (acquired in 1925)
Clark Field II (1928)
G.I. Halls (1947-1973)
Deep Eddy Apartments (1948)

Buildings still in use

Dorothy Gebauer Student Service Building (1904)
    [Vacant since 1992]
Battle Hall (1911)
Sutton Hall (1917)
Texas Memorial Stadium (1924)
Biological Laboratories (1925)
Heman Sweatt Campus (acquired in 1926)
        Arno Nowotny Building
        John W. Hargis Hall
Garrison Hall (1926)
Littlefield Dormitory (1927)
Hal C. Weaver Power Plant (1928)
Gregory Gymnasium (1930)
Anna Hiss Gymnasium (1931)
Welch Hall (1931 and 1978)
Waggener Hall (1931)
Brackenridge Hall (1932)
Goldsmith Hall (1933)
Taylor Hall (1928-1934)
Gearing Hall (1933)
Will C. Hogg Building (1933)
Painter Hall (1933)
Texas Union (1933)
Education Annex (1933)
Hogg Memorial Auditorium (1933)
Littlefield Home and Carriage House (acquired in 1935)
Roberts Hall (1936)
Andrews Dormitory (1936)
Prather Hall (1937)
Carothers Hall (1937)
Main Building and Tower (1933-1937)
Texas Memorial Museum (1937)
Moore-Hill Hall (1939 and 1955)
E. P. Schoch Building (1942)
Economics Building (1942)
Brackenridge Apartments I and II (1947 and 1980s)
Student Health Center (1950)
Experimental Science Building (1951)
Women's Cooperatives (1952 and 1969)
Pharmacy Building (1952)

Batts Hall (1952)

Mezes Hall (1952)

Benedict Hall (1952)

Geography Building (1952)

Service Building (1952)

Townes Hall and Jesse H. Jones Hall [Law School]
(1953-1981)

Mobile Home Park (1955)

Simkins Hall (1955)

Blanton Dormitory (1955)

Varsity Center (1955)

Parlin Hall (1956)

Russell A. Steindam Hall and Rifle Range (1957)

Kinsolving Dormitory (1958)

W. R. Woolrich Laboratories (1958)

University Police Building (1960)

Computation Center (1961)

West Mall Office Building (1962)

F. Loren Winship Drama Building (1962)

College of Business Administration Building (1962)

Peter T. Flawn Academic Center (1963)

Art Building (1963)

Engineering Science Building (1964)

Etter-Neuhaus Alumni Center (1965 and 1990)

Office building: 2617 Speedway (acquired in 1966)

Colorado Apartments (1966)

Whitaker Field (1966)

Wooldridge Hall (acquired in 1966)

Office building: 200 East 26 1/2 Street (acquired in 1967)

Brackenridge Field Laboratory (1967)

Geology Building (1967)

Graduate and International Admissions Center
(acquired in 1967)

Bridgeway (acquired in 1968)

Personnel Building (acquired in 1968)

Social Work Building (acquired in 1968)

Office Building: 2601 University Avenue
(acquired in 968)

Office building: 2622 Wichita Street (acquired in 1968)

Office building: 100 East 26th Street (acquired in 1968)

Calhoun Hall (1968)

Collections Deposit Library (1968)
Beauford H. Jester Center (1969)
Music Building East (1969)
Patterson Laboratories Building (1969)
Office building: 107 West 27th Street (acquired in 1970)
Thompson Conference Center (1970)
Burdine Hall (1970)
Sid Richardson Hall (1971)
Lyndon Baines Johnson Library and Museum (1971)
L. Theo Bellmont Hall (1972)
Robert Lee Moore Hall (1972)
Walter Webb Hall (acquired in 1972)
Harry Ransom Center (1973)
Walter Webb Hall (acquired in 1972)
Central Receiving Building (1973)
Jesse H. Jones Communication Center (1973)
Gateway Apartments (1973)
Nursing Building (1973)
Ernest Cockrell, Jr., Hall (1974)
Clark Field III (1974)
Disch-Falk Field (1975)
College of Education Building (1975)
Graduate School of Business Building (1976)
Perry-Castaneda Library (1977)
Frank C. Erwin Special Events Center (1977)
Printing and Press Building (1977)
Lee and Joe Jamail Texas Swimming Center (1977)
Animal Resources Center (1977)
Fine Arts Complex and Performing Arts Center
    (1979-1981)
    Bass Concert Hall (1981)
    Music Building and Bates Recital Hall (1980)
    Ralph and Ruth McCullough Theatre (1980)
    Drama Workshops (1980)
    Fine Arts Library and Administration Building (1979)
Engineering Teaching Center II (1983)
University Teaching Center (1984)
Penick-Allison Tennis Center (1986)
Neuhaus-Royal Athletic Center (1986)
Parking Garage I (1986)
Physical Plant Complex (1967-1991)

Recreational Sports Center (1990)
Parking Garage II (1993)

Under construction
Molecular Biology Building
Student Services Building
Parking Garage III

UT MAP

AND BUILDING INDEX

THE UNIVERSITY OF TEXAS AT AUSTIN

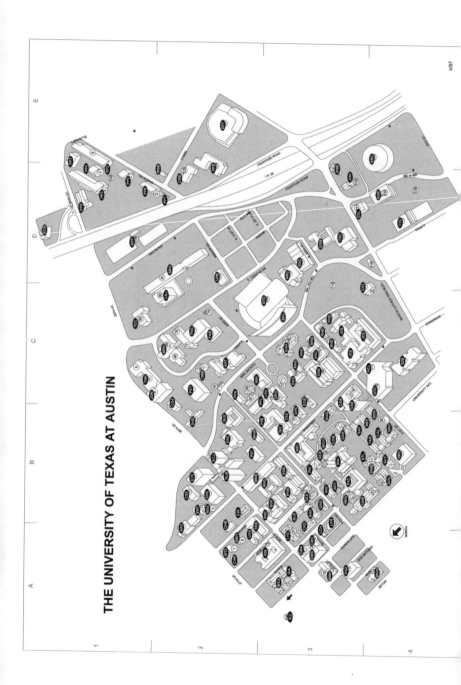

111

Engineering Teaching Center II: ETC, 17, B-2

Frank C. Erwin, Jr. Special Events Center: ERC, 134, E-4

Lila B. Etter Alumni Center: EAH, 104, C-3

Experimental Science Building: ESB, 30, B-3

F

Peter T. Flawn Academic Center: FAC ,53 ,B-3

Fine Arts Library and Administration Building: FAB, 75, C-2

Charles I. Francis Auditorium: TNH, 47b, C-1

G

Garrison Hall: GAR, 94, B-3

Mary E. Gearing Hall: GEA, 29, B-3

Dorothy Gebauer (Building closed): GEB, 58, B-3

Geography Building: GRG, 24, B-3

Geology Building: GEO, 70, C-3

Goldsmith Hall: GOL, 82, B-4

Gregory Gymnasium: GRE, 99, C-3

Guard Station (UT Police): H

H

John W. Hargis Hall: JHH, 132, D-3

Hill Hall Dormitory: HHD, 103, C-3

Anna Hiss Gymnasium: AHG, 34, B-3

Hogg Memorial Auditorium: HMA, 52, B-3

Will C. Hogg Building: WCH, 59, B-3

Office of Human Resources (Personnel Office): OHR, 11, B-2

Huntington Art Gallery in the Art Building: ART, 74, C-2

Huntington Art Gallery in the Harry Ransom Center: HRC, 83, B-4

J

Lee and Joe Jamail Texas Swimming Center: TSC, 123, D-3

Beauford H. Jester Center: JES, 113, C-3

Lyndon B. Johnson Auditorium: LBJ, 80, C-2

Lyndon B. Johnson School of Public Affairs: SRH, 81, D-2

Lyndon Baines Johnson Library and Museum: LBJ, 80, C-2

Jesse H. Jones Communication Center: CMA, CMB, CMC, 20a-c, A-3

Jesse H. Jones Hall: JON, 47a, C-2

K

Kinsolving Dormitory: KIN, 3, A-3

George Kozmetsky Center: GSB, CBA, 96, 97, C-3 , for Business Education: UTC, 110, C-4

L

Laboratory Theatre Building: LTH, 71, C-3

Littlefield Carriage House: LCH, 22, A-3

Littlefield Dormitory: LTD, 27, A-3

Littlefield Fountain: 90, B-4

Littlefield Home: LFH, 23, B-3

M

Main Building and Tower: MAI, 56, B-3

Ralph and Ruth McCullough Theatre: PAC, 78, C-2

Mezes Hall: MEZ, 92, B-3

Moffett Molecular Biology Building: MMB, 35, B-3

Moore Hall Dormitory: MHD, 103, C-3

Robert Lee Moore Hall: RLM, 38, B-2

INDEX

115

116

118

123